THE DIVINE
AND MASTER ZHANG

THE
DIVINE
AND MASTER ZHANG

The Astonishing Life and Powers of
Spiritual Healer Zhang Ying

TANYA HARTER PIERCE

Blue Stone Productions
Austin, Texas

Copyright © 2019 Blue Stone Productions, LLC
Printed and Bound in the United States of America

All rights reserved. No part of this book may be used or reproduced, stored in a retrieval system or transmitted, in any form or by any means—electronic, mechanical, photocopying, recording or otherwise—without prior permission from the publisher, except for the inclusion of brief quotations in a review.

The Divine and Master Zhang:
The Astonishing Life and Powers of Spiritual Healer Zhang Ying

Published by Blue Stone Productions, LLC
Austin, Texas
Publisher Contact: Kathy@Equifoal.com

This book is the true account of the life and talents of Chinese healer, Master Zhang Ying, as shared by her with the author. It is for personal and educational use only and nothing in this work should be construed as medical advice.
The author and publisher have made every effort to ensure the accuracy of information contained in this book, however they do not assume responsibility for any inaccuracies due to translation errors from Chinese to English. To protect the privacy of people mentioned in this book, some names have been changed. Any slights of people, places, or organizations are unintentional.

ISBN: 978-1-7335007-0-8 (Paperback)
ISBN: 978-1-7335007-1-5 (Digital Book)

Front Cover Design by Roger Reyes
Photo Images Courtesy of Master Zhang Ying
Typesetting and Interior Design by www.1106design.com

Acknowledgments

FIRST AND FOREMOST, I would like to express my deep gratitude to Master Zhang for sharing her life story and entrusting me with the honor of presenting it to the world for the first time in English. She specified virtually no restrictions as to how to organize this book about her, and she also displayed great patience when there were delays. I am convinced that Master Zhang is a very important person for all of humanity, though I am not qualified to know the broad extent of all she has to offer or what all her roles may eventually be. She often refers to *the heavens* when speaking of the Divine, and my sense is that "the heavens" have cared about Master Zhang very much since the day she was born. There is no higher acclaim that I can give her.

I would also like to express my sincere appreciation to Kathy and Steve Shubin for the key roles they played in helping to produce this book, particularly in the later production phases. Without their involvement, it may not have come together at all. And I want to thank Kim R. Holland and Suzy Yu Zhang for giving generously of their time as interpreters so I could interview Master Zhang on many occasions and communicate with her regarding publication matters as they came up. Their help was and still is greatly appreciated. Finally, I would like to thank Rui Cao for her translation work, especially with the photo captions, and Deborah Harter for her creative input.

There have been others along the way who helped as well, and to all who contributed, I extend my sincere appreciation and acknowledgment that we all, quite simply, did it for Master Zhang.

Table of Contents

Acknowledgments   v
Introduction   xiii
Notes to Readers   xxi

— The Trials of Growing Up —

Chapter 1   An Unusual Child   3

       Dragon Birth
       Seeing the Future
       The Big-Hearted Zhang Benxue
       The Surprising Satchel

Chapter 2   Entering Society   17

       The Other Side of Coma
       A Vision and Rescue

Chapter 3	Training Commences	25
	Meditation and Hand Stamps	
	Sleeping ABOVE the Bed	
	First Attempt at Healing	
Chapter 4	Struggling to Be a Healer	33
	Marriage	
	Tornado	
	The Lady in Blue	
	Pills From the Buddha	
Chapter 5	The Year Without Sun	45
	Into the River	
	Arrested Again	
Chapter 6	FIRE	49
	A Net From Heaven	
	The Spirit Master Returns	
	More Divine Powers	
Chapter 7	Finally Dead	59
	Strange Things	
	A Name Change	
	Her Earthly Master Arrives	
Chapter 8	Service Home for the Aged	69
	An Old Woman's Plight	

Table of Contents

— Official Testing and New Powers —

Chapter 9	Testing Begins	81
	The I & R Team	
	Treating at a Distance	
Chapter 10	Going to Beijing	89
	Ms. Zeng	
	Controlled Conditions and Cameras	
	Grabbing Medicine From the Air	
Chapter 11	Raining Medicine	123
	The Ren Couple	
	Pill Within a Pill	
	Liquid Medicine	
	Miracle at the Pagoda	
Chapter 12	International Recognition	131
	Huge Audiences	
	Girl With BB Bullet in Her Eye	
	Boy with Myasthenia Gravis	
	Blind Boy Says, "It's a Tiger!"	
	Nun Photographed in White Light	
	Postman Vomits Up Cancer	

Chapter 13 Communicating with Spirits 145

    Talking to the Raven
    The Wandering Emperor's Spirit
    A Visit from Kuan Yin
    Two Encounters with Jesus Christ

Chapter 14 Pearls, Turtles, and Teleportations 155

    Pearls for Everyone
    Three Turtles Appear
    Ancient Buried Coins
    Getting Change
    Two Flasks of Water
    Money Materializes

Chapter 15 Trouble in Taiwan 167

    Media Craze and TV Show
    Unfair Detention
    Pills in the Courtroom

Chapter 16 Coming to America 175

    The Spirit Wolf and Black-Haired Guide
    Severe Edema
    A Headless Demon and Spider Spirit
    A Vindictive Mother Spirit
    Snakes Seek Revenge
    Tumor Jumps Into Hand
    Jade Turtles Everywhere

Table of Contents

— In Master Zhang's Own Words —

Chapter 17   Interview with Master Zhang   199

    Daily Life
    Angels, Spirit Guides, and Dragons
    Animals and Nature Spirits
    Karma and God

Chapter 18   Mysteries of the Universe   213

    Wave of Life
    Time and Information From the Universe
    Pre-Prediction and Post-Prediction
    Bioelectric Current (Chi)
    The Holographic Cell
    Idea Moving (Teleportation)
    More About "Strange Things"

Chapter 19   Strange Prescriptions   225

    Wild Scorpions to Cure Stomach Cancer
    Seven-Star Spiders to Cure Cancer
    Bronze Thimble to Cure Epilepsy
    Other Prescriptions from Heaven

Chapter 20   The Work Continues   233

    Global Connections
    Spiritual Healing in the United States

Appendix   Curious Similarities: A Brief Comparison
            of Paranormal Abilities   239
   Special Gifts
   Levitation
   Strange Prescriptions and Distant Diagnosing
   Miraculous Healings
   Rising From the Dead
   Manifesting Objects Out of the Air

Introduction

—ɷ—

*I*T WAS HIGHLY UNLIKELY I would ever meet Master Zhang or be able to write a book about her. She speaks only Chinese, while I speak only English. She does not advertise her services at all. And we live in different parts of the United States. The likelihood I would ever even *hear* about her was extremely low. Nevertheless, a series of events led us to meet and to eventually finalize this book about her astounding life and abilities. At first, I was amazed at how these events fell into place. In hindsight, they appeared to have been destined. Much later, after getting to know Master Zhang better, I began to believe there was probably nothing in this remarkable woman's life that was *not* destined.

When I first traveled to southern California for a healing session with Master Zhang, I was excited to have the opportunity to meet and observe this enigmatic healer. I had heard amazing things about what she could do and was pretty sure she would be able to see inside my body and know everything about me, both physically and personally. I must admit, I was more than a little nervous. Not that I had anything in particular to hide . . . but still, it was a strange and slightly unsettling situation to be in.

I had been escorted into a very nice home in an attractive southern California neighborhood. The setting was pleasant, yet at the same time, it also felt odd. It would have seemed much more appropriate to have spent weeks traveling to a high mountaintop temple in the Himalayas in order to meet such a healer reveared by many, who I was already beginning to think of as a *phenomenon*. Nevertheless, there I was, in suburban California.

I was initially surprised by how Master Zhang presented herself as just an ordinary person. She greeted me warmly and in casual attire, wearing slippers (in the Chinese tradition of not wearing outdoor shoes indoors) and a sweatshirt to ward off the chill of the morning air. What struck me as exceptional, however, were her eyes. Somehow, whenever she smiled, light seemed to shine out of them, and this had an extraordinary effect on me that I could not explain.

Another woman had been scheduled for a session before me and I was permitted to observe. I watched as Master Zhang used her "x-ray vision" to look into the woman's body, described the condition and functioning of her internal organs, and considered her energy flow. This was done in a style of diagnosing that was not western, but was rather Chinese, and was achieved with the help of an expert interpreter. At the end of the session, Master Zhang appeared to focus inwardly and held up both hands around eye level in front of her. She made some unusual formations with her fingers and a few moments later told the interpreter to have the woman cup her hands beneath hers. She then started sifting a brown powder between her thumb and forefinger into the woman's hands! *She had just caused a healing herbal powder to materialize for the woman right*

Introduction

out of the air. A few moments later, *an herbal pill materialized right out of the air as well!*

My turn was next and I couldn't help wondering if my own session would be as exciting. I was not disappointed. Master Zhang told me about the condition and functioning of my internal organs and remarked on a childhood injury to my head that had occurred when I was about three years old. That surprised me, but I was even more astonished when she explained that, when my husband and I had cut down some trees in our backyard five years earlier, this had allowed some malevolent spirits to negatively impact us, perhaps contributing to the breakdown of our marriage a few years later. I had not previously told her about the cutting down of the trees. And certainly on hearing from her that they had somehow protected us from these spirits, I decided never to cut down a tree again.

Finally, at the end of my session, I watched Master Zhang rub her thumb and forefinger together and saw a light-brown powder fall from between her fingers into the palm of my hand! There was no trickery, no misdirection, and no long sleeves or pockets where something could be secretly hidden and pulled out with sleight of hand. There were simply Master Zhang's very obviously empty hands making some strange movements in the air, after which I was told to cup my own hands under hers to catch the powder.

This was clearly the most fascinating person I'd ever met! What kept going through my mind was that *anyone who can do THAT knows a lot more about reality than the rest of us.*

Being a writer and having heard about the extraordinary things this healer could do, I had entertained the idea of writing a book about her. I would never have mentioned this to her on our first meeting, of course, but I did say that I was feeling very stressed due to my divorce and was concerned about my business and future financial security. Master Zhang asked me what my business was and I told her I'd written a book on alternative non-toxic cancer treatments titled *Outsmart Your Cancer*, which I had been selling for eight years at that point. Her reply was entirely unexpected. "You should write a book about how I help people with cancer!" she exclaimed. I was thrilled and told her I would love to do so, but I also wondered at her having been so quick to give someone she hardly knew permission to write about her. Later, I learned that Master Zhang often psychically knows a great deal more about a person than they realize, even sometimes before she meets them. In fact, she revealed to me that, on the morning of my session, one of her animal spirit guides had appeared to her in a dream and told her she was going to meet someone that day who would be able to help her to help more people.

After my session, I asked Master Zhang through the interpreter if Kuan Yin, a divine being in Buddhism, gave her the medicine she so regularly caused to materialize out of the air. Master Zhang shook her head to indicate "No." She then pointed toward a poster on her wall of the Medicine Buddha, another divine being who is considered the highest possible representation of a healer in Buddhism. Master Zhang was telling me it was the Medicine Buddha who provided her with the powders and pills she manifested for her clients. I was later told that it could either be the Medicine Buddha, Kuan Yin, or some other high-level spirit being. The powder can be dark brown or light tan, and the herbal pills can be brown, black, red, or even gold. Sometimes, Master Zhang can even materialize a powerful *liquid* herbal medicine that drips from her hands into cups or bowls held out by those she treats. Clearly, I had a lot to learn!

Introduction

I'd just seen pills and powders materialize out of thin air in my own session and during those of others, and I felt like I had slipped down the rabbit hole in *Alice in Wonderland*. I noticed that my mind was strangely blank. It was as if I were looking for thoughts that could make sense of what I had just seen . . . but there weren't any! When I left that day carrying my small envelope of brown herbal powder that had come from God knows where, I was somewhat giddy. It would have been an understatement to say that I was dazzled by Master Zhang. In my hotel room later that evening, there seemed to be a tangible message in the air around me that was literally telling me, *there's going to be a BIG change in your life!* This message did not feel like it was coming from any particular entity, but rather more like it was a general message from the universe. And indeed a big change did happen, as I embarked on the journey of this project.

This first English account of Master Zhang's life began when she allowed me to interview her personally, providing me as well with both published and unpublished written material about her from China. The best written source of information at the time, and from which much of the quoted text in this book originates, was an unpublished memoir, in which Master Zhang had recorded many of the events of her life and career. It had been roughly translated into English and proved extremely helpful as a source of details regarding Master Zhang's childhood, how she was officially tested, and some of her more memorable healing cases. Another book from China, had not been translated into English, but had excellent photos and is titled, *Spiritual Light: A Collection of Cases Where Master Zhang Uses Her Special Abilities to Cure People* (by Jianxin Li and Qin Zheng, Inner Mongolian Publishing Company, 1998). I was able to obtain permission to use some of the photos from this book.

THE DIVINE AND MASTER ZHANG

I was particularly pleased to see that *Spiritual Light* presented, not just photos of Master Zhang posing with government and military leaders (and a variety of other high-ranking officials) as well as with famous qigong masters, but also in which she was giving healing demonstrations in front of extremely large crowds. Master Zhang provided me with other photos as well, and these, along with my continued observations of her work with others, made me keenly aware that making herbal powders and pills materialize out of thin air was just one of Master Zhang's many talents. Her uncommon abilities are far-reaching, and include interacting with spirits, teleporting items from one place to another, seeing inside people's bodies, diagnosing at a distance, and coming up with rare and strange prescriptions, which are unusual remedies transmitted to Master Zhang directly from the spirit world. Many times, these simply come into her mind quite suddenly, along with instructions on how to use them. For example, a case is presented in Chapter 19 where Master Zhang helped achieve a cure for someone in China with stomach cancer by suggesting a remedy made from wild scorpions. It was quite interesting to me later to find out that cancer patients have been traveling to Cuba since the 1980s to be treated with an alternative remedy made from Blue Scorpion venom! Master Zhang explains her talents in the following way:

> The reason I can perceive those strange things as well as rare prescriptions, is essentially that I have psychic powers endowed by nature, which loves life. Nature takes advantage of my psychic powers to free people from pain and suffering.

Even though an abundance of case stories and other phenomenal events are presented in this book, it must be said that they are

Introduction

only a fraction of the countless healings and incredible happenings that Master Zhang has been a part of over her lifetime. In all her healing work in China, she helped anyone she could who came to her in need, and she did not charge those who were poor. All of this while being persecuted by local authorities, and even at times beaten up or thrown in jail by the Chinese communist regime that was determined at the time to stamp out all spiritual activities.

One thing is certain. Very few can claim to have had such a fascinating life as Master Zhang has had. Her story reads at first like a fairy tale replete with dragons, spirit guides, visions, miracles, and teleportations. Gradually, it becomes more and more real, however, as her powers are tested by scientists, hailed by qigong masters, and witnessed by thousands as they watch her give demonstrations. It is astonishing that such an extraordinary life has remained so unknown to those of us in the West.

When asked about her vision for this book, Master Zhang explained that she hoped more than anything that it would present "stories of the heart." In other words, it was particularly important to her that she be able to share real-life cases from her work where various people she'd helped had their hearts and minds opened. I have certainly tried to fulfill this wish. But I must say that, given how cruelly Master Zhang was treated in her own life, and how she had to persevere through great hardship to help people in need, for me, there is no story with more heart in it than her own. The remarkable, true account of this amazing woman's life—from poor village girl to famous healer—begins in Chapter 1.

— TANYA HARTER PIERCE

Notes to Readers

—ɷ—

NOTE #1. CHINESE NAMES. In Chinese, a person's last name is always spoken or written first. Thus, Master Zhang's surname (pronounced "ZHONG") is expressed first throughout this book; then her first name, "Ying," follows. "Master Zhang," or "Master Zhang Ying," are both formal and respectful ways to address her. Other Chinese names conform to the same rule. Thus, Wang Shikuai is a man whose last name is Wang and first name is Shikuai, and Xiao Fen is a woman whose last name is Xiao and first name is Fen.

NOTE #2. SHUXIA TO YING. As will be shown in upcoming chapters, Ying is not the first name Master Zhang was originally given as a child. She was originally named "Shuxia" (pronounced "SHOO-sya," with emphasis on the first syllable), and the story of her early life will be told using this informal first name. She later changed her first name to Ying (pronounced "ING"), making her current full name "Zhang Ying."

NOTE #3. GODS and GODDESSES. These are sometimes referred to in the text because the concept of many deities is common in Buddhism, the predominant spiritual discipline of China. However, it is important to understand this does not mean Buddhism is a polytheistic religion of many gods in the western sense. Rather, in Buddhism, gods, goddesses, or deities are seen as representing the various wonderful divine attributes of the one God. In both Buddhism and Hinduism, these deities may also represent aspects of the infinite within each of us that, when focused upon through devotional acts, may help seekers to cultivate those qualities within themselves.

NOTE #4. KUAN YIN. Kuan Yin is considered a Bodhisattva in Buddhism (pronounced "Bod-ee-SOT-vuh"). The spelling of Kuan Yin's name in English varies from Kuan Yin or Kwan Yin to Guan Yin or Guanyin. Bodhisattvas may also be referred to as Buddhas themselves, or as aspects of the one Buddha. Thus, someone might appropriately refer to Kuan Yin as a Bodhisattva, or as the Kuan Yin Buddha, or as Kuan Yin "Pusa," which is merely closer to the Chinese pronunciation of their word for Buddha. These are all correct. Kuan Yin is widely revered as the beloved Bodhisattva of Compassion who "hears the cries of the world." She is also referred to as the Goddess of Mercy.

Notes to Readers

NOTE #5. DRAGONS. Dragons are often referred to in Chinese culture, and this can be confusing to the western reader. In China, dragons are thought of as some aspect of spirit incarnated on Earth. They are not seen as bad things, as in the western world, but as good things. In fact, it is common for dragons to be looked at as auspicious (positive) signs of God at work.

NOTE #6. CHI. In traditional Chinese philosophy and medicine, "chi" is the vital energy of the body and must be balanced and flowing without blockages for good health. This vital force is referred to as "chi" in China, "qi" in Japan and "prana" in India. On the simplest level, chi is seen as a dynamic system of interrelating forces composed of "yin" chi and "yang" chi. However, in China, the understanding of chi is much more complicated and detailed than this. Those who are highly skilled at understanding and working with chi, such as Master Zhang, can identify many sub-forms and characteristics of chi. In modern-day Asia, numerous scientific studies on chi have been performed that have proven its existence and defined some of the characteristics of this vital energy. Though some electromagnetic and other scientifically understood characteristics have been discovered, there are still aspects of chi that modern science has yet to explain. This may be because chi is more than just a form of energy with physical characteristics—it also appears to carry information. For this reason, chi is sometimes referred to as "intelligent energy."

NOTE #7. QIGONG. (Also spelled Chi Gong or Chi Gung.) Qigong refers to the practice of moving and working with chi. For thousands of years, advanced practitioners in Asia have learned to master this art with the aid of controlled breath and thought. Most qigong practice is directed at moving and balancing the energy inside one's own body, resulting in better health and even spiritual enlightenment. But advanced masters can also emit "external" chi toward people who are sick for healing purposes. Qigong is the basis upon which acupuncture, tai chi, and oriental martial arts were developed, and those who are referred to as "Qigong Masters" are generally the most highly skilled at working with chi.

There is a connection between things that are in form and things that are formless. . . . When body, mind, and spirit are balanced, anything is possible.

— Master Zhang Ying

— THE TRIALS OF GROWING UP —

Chapter 1

An Unusual Child

—⚏—

Dragon Birth

ONE DAY, A BABY GIRL WAS about to be born in the small village of Xiaoyingzi in the Liaoning province of northeast China. The young mother already thought there might be something special about this fifth child because she had felt so much better than she had during her four previous pregnancies. In fact, ailments that had plagued her for years strangely vanished while carrying this baby. The mother's name was Du Lanrong, and she was preparing to give birth at home.

The weather had become more and more unusual that day. It was sunny on one side of the sky, while dark with heavy rainfall on the other. The baby was just about ready to arrive. Suddenly, something that looked like black smoke bolted down from the heavens amidst thunder and lightning, flew into the birthing room shattering the window as it entered, and swiftly flew around in a circle over

Du Lanrong. Then, it went back out the window as a ball of fire! A moment later, the little girl was born.

Alarmed neighbors, after hearing the window shatter and seeing the black smoke, came running over thinking the house was on fire. But of course it wasn't. Strangely, the young mother was calm. She felt she had been visited by a black dragon, which to her was a very good omen. Her upbringing had taught her that animals—whether real or mythical—were used as symbols of certain traits or concepts. Dragons were always considered the *highest* representation of power and luck, which was why through much of China's long history, only emperors were allowed to take the name of a dragon or wear images of dragons on their clothing. Du Lanrong knew that dragons were considered the highest animal form of spirit incarnated on Earth. She also knew that dragons were always from Heaven. Yes, it was a very good omen.

The newborn was named Shuxia (pronounced "SHOO-sya"). She turned out to be a very happy baby whom everyone liked. But for some reason, she had very dark skin, much darker than anyone else in her family. Her skin color lightened quite a bit as she grew older, but while young, she was called, "the little black girl." None of her older siblings or the three younger sisters she would later have had this dark skin color, and some have wondered if this was related to the black dragon that came in through the window just as she was born.

Shuxia's mother, Du Lanrong, was tall, elegantly beautiful, and had been born into a rather rich family. She had grown up the daughter of a landlord and was very cultured. She'd even studied some of the classic literature. But her own mother had passed away when she was young, and her stepmother did not like her. As a result, she was married off to a poor commoner without any care for the hardship this would cause her.

An Unusual Child

Thus, Du Lanrong had been forced to marry Shuxia's father, Zhang Benxue (pronounced "ZHONG ben-Shway"). Zhang Benxue was a good man. But he was extremely poor, six years older than his wife, short and small in stature. Overall, he was of undistinguished appearance. Because of having to marry such a poor man, Du Lanrong was sentenced to a difficult life. She felt wronged and never went back to visit her father or stepmother again.

But overall, Du Lanrong was a good woman. It was just that China was going through very hard economic times and her new life was one of stark poverty. Her husband had to find odd jobs and work in the fields as well as take on carpentry work to eke out a very poor existence. The family had raised several chickens and one dog, but that was all they had. Good food was not always available year round and they subsisted mainly on corn buns, kaoliang gruels, and salted vegetables.

Green vegetables were rarely on the table and Shuxia's mother always felt bad that her children had to make do with so little. She often quarreled with her husband when the children weren't around. As a result of stress and unhappiness, this once beautiful woman had become thin and worn to a shadow by the time she was pregnant with her fifth child. She looked more like a fifty-year-old woman than someone in the prime of her life. She had also thought of committing suicide more than once. But when she was five or six months pregnant with Shuxia, Du Lanrong experienced a vision. In the vision, she saw the door to a temple open up and heard a voice say to her,

> Do you still want to die? What about the four children you have now and the one inside you? In the future, you will be very well-respected and taken care of.

THE DIVINE AND MASTER ZHANG

So Du Lanrong did not commit suicide or have an abortion as she had considered. She trusted her vision. Luckily, as her pregnancy developed, she felt better and better physically and mentally. Later, she told her daughter Shuxia,

> When I had you in my pregnancy, my health had become very poor, and I worried very much about this pregnancy. Several times I thought about abortion. However, I finally made up my mind to have you, because no child should have to suffer from the poverty of the mother. Let it be with destiny. Strangely enough, while you were in my womb, I became rejuvenated. Everybody who saw me would say that I had become fresh in appearance and strong in my health. *Oh, my elder sister, what kind of good nutrition have you had that makes you look so bright?* they would remark.
>
> Once I was dozing off to sleep and it seemed that in the western sky there happened to be a bright lightning, like a fireball. I thought it must be the Goddess of Mercy bringing brightness and hope. I felt so open-minded and did not think of committing suicide after that.
>
> I remember clearly the day of your birth. It was in 1962, the second of August of the Chinese lunar year. Since then, I have always been healthy and suffered no illnesses. I think it was you bringing me luck. It's really our fate. Your birth got rid of all my sufferings and illnesses. Maybe you were born to be an angel to resolve the pain and suffering of others.

Of course, little Shuxia was too young to understand her fate.

Shuxia's family lived in a rural area near the Dalinghe River at the base of Nuluerhu Mountain. Their village was a place of mixed heritage, with more than one hundred Han and Mongolian households, and Shuxia's family came from Mongolian ancestry. Like many others in her village, they were very poor. Much of the time, her father made only the equivalent of about five cents a day. Shuxia's mother would make clothes for the oldest daughter, which would then be handed down to the next oldest daughter. By the time Shuxia was big enough to wear the hand-me-downs, they were falling apart, so her mother made new clothes for her. These were then handed down and worn by her three younger sisters, who unfortunately often ended up with shoes that had their toes worn out.

But none of this early poverty bothered Shuxia at all. As a child, she exhibited a kind heart and inherent goodness, and serving others came naturally to her. For instance, even though she was poor, she would sometimes take what food she could, such as salted vegetables in a jar, from her own household and give it away to a poorer villager. She would not pay attention to her family members if they complained. Once, Shuxia saw an old villager smoking his pipe with grass in it because he was too poor to buy tobacco. So she stealthily plucked some of the tobacco leaves from her own family's garden and gave them to the old man.

Seeing the Future

Shuxia was not only kind-hearted, though. It soon became apparent that she was different from other children in some very unusual ways. She could see what others could not see and often predicted events that would happen in the future. As an example, when she was only seven, a villager named Wang Shikuai, who was a little older than Shuxia's father, was a frequent visitor to her family. One day Wang came to their home and told her parents that he liked

Shuxia very much and wanted to adopt her as his daughter. He had always thought Shuxia was special because of the dragon omen at her birth. Since her own family was so poor, this was a chance for a better life for Shuxia. Her parents were delighted and went to look for Shuxia, who had hidden in the courtyard. Her mother found her and tried to get her to accept the offer, saying,

> My third daughter, your Uncle Wang would like to adopt you as his daughter. It's really wonderful! Why not just go there and call him "father"?
> *No, I'm afraid of him,* Shuxia said.
> Why? He likes you very much and can provide you an opportunity to study at school and to buy you pretty clothes.
> *I do not like it. You should see by his belly that is so big and his face that looks terrible that he might not live long.*

Shuxia's mother was stunned by the response her seven-year-old daughter gave. After recovering from her surprise she said, "Don't talk nonsense. How can that be? Doesn't he look good right now?"

But Shuxia would not give in and she stayed with her parents. Less than two months later, Wang Shikuai died of ascites from liver disease. Just before his death, his belly became really big and his face looked really terrible.

The next year, when she was eight, little Shuxia saw the butcher of her village and commented that he looked like he had been suffocated to death. Her mother said, "He is a man living a happy life! How can he be suffocated to death? Don't talk such nonsense."

Shuxia replied with confidence, "It's real and I have seen it." Shortly afterward, the man died from convulsions.

An Unusual Child

Another time, when Shuxia was a teenager, her mother took her and one of her older sisters out to a field to cut grass. Shuxia looked up and saw two people walking by, one of whom was a girl about her own age. Shuxia whispered to her mother that the girl was walking around with a baby in her belly. As the pregnancy was not far enough along to show, and no one else in the village knew about it, Shuxia's mother said, "She is only 14 years old. How can she be pregnant? Don't say that and don't make a scene!"

Later, they learned the girl had gotten an abortion when she was about six months pregnant.

The Big-Hearted Zhang Benxue

Shuxia's beloved father, Zhang Benxue, was primarily a carpenter. He was well known and very well liked in her village. Though small in physique, he was praised by the villagers as a "big" man due to his charity and kind-hearted character. He often did carpentry work for fellow villagers for free if they couldn't afford to pay, and whenever he worked outside his village he would only charge a reasonable fee or ask for a donation. Thus, he never earned much money for his own family. Zhang Benxue was extremely amiable and never once hit or blamed his children, as some other fathers did. He also never took the life of an animal. On the contrary, he used to buy captive fish or birds from others and set them free.

Shuxia's father greatly influenced her as she grew up. One of the events that made a deep impression on her occurred several days before the Dragon festival in the 1980s. Zhang Benxue had just come home tired after working in the fields and lay down to rest. He fell asleep and dreamed he heard someone shouting, "Help! Help!" In his dream, he looked and saw a white-haired, white-mustached old man running and crying out for assistance. When he tried to do something to help the man, he woke up. He was so puzzled by this strange dream that he went outside and walked around, trying to understand it. Shortly, he came upon a villager who was returning from fishing in the nearby river. The villager was carrying a bamboo basket filled with fish and a bowl-sized turtle.

Somehow, Shuxia's father knew that the white-mustached old man of his dream was crying out for help for this turtle. He asked the villager to sell the turtle to him, but the villager did not want to give up such a tasty dish for his dinner. After negotiating some more, Zhang Benxue was eventually able to persuade the man to let him buy the turtle. He had to run back home and get seven eggs and several coins to make the purchase, which was quite a large sacrifice for him, but he finally got the turtle in hand. Then, he promptly set it free back into the river. After swimming a few meters, the turtle turned its head around to look at Shuxia's father. It seemed to be expressing gratitude and some reluctance to depart. Finally, the turtle happily swam off into deep water.

Another event that strongly impacted Shuxia was a story her father once shared with her and her siblings. Zhang Benxue told them,

> One night in 1969—as I remember, it was the December Chinese lunar year—your grandpa had a very strange dream. He saw a man in the dream dressed in a long gown with a yellow vest different from the modern style of clothes. The man said in a serious but kind way to your grandpa, *Here comes someone from the above authority,* and he asked me to bring the family a horizontal inscription. The inscription was

An Unusual Child

on a yellow brocade [woven fabric] three *chi* wide [the unit *chi* is approximately one foot long], with red embroidered characters. Your grandpa asked what the red embroidered characters were. The man answered, *They are a blessing from the Almighty God.* He also said, *You can drape it over only one of your family members.* At that time, grandpa saw only you [Shuxia], so he draped the yellow brocade over your shoulders. When grandpa wanted to ask more about the meaning of it all, the man had vanished.

After telling this to the children, Zhang Benxue smiled at Shuxia and said, "So, you are lucky to have a direct blessing from God."

Zhang Benxue was a very hardworking man. During a time when China was advocating a system of family responsibility for land cultivation, he opened up an area of wasteland on a river bank. The crops he planted in this wasteland included wheat and corn and they produced good harvests every year, even when there were floods and the other villagers lost their crops and went hungry. Sometimes he could get good harvests before the floods occurred. So, everyone in the village used to say that Shuxia's family was blessed and they would imitate her father's cultivation style. They would seed what her family seeded and harvest when her family harvested. This way, the other villagers also got good harvests in succession for several years.

Once, Shuxia's mother told her that two fortune tellers had predicted her father would only live to the age of forty-three. When he did reach forty-three, he was helping another villager cut down a large tree. Suddenly, the tree started falling in such a direction, he thought it would surely land on him and kill him quickly. But at the last moment, it seemed as if someone pushed Zhang Benxue out of the way and he escaped the danger. That night, he dreamed of the white-mustached old man again. The old man was smiling at Zhang Benxue and said, "Throughout your life, you have done a lot of charitable things and have accumulated merits. So you will have thirty-seven *more* years of life."

The old man in the dream then disappeared and Zhang Benxue woke up. What the white-mustached man said came true. He died exactly thirty-seven years later at the age of eighty. Zhang Benxue had dedicated his whole life to doing charitable deeds and cared deeply about all living things. His attitude toward life had a profound influence on Shuxia.

When Shuxia was a little more than ten years old, her mother asked a fortune-teller about her. The fortune-teller said that Shuxia had a pattern on her palm indicating she would be a talented general. Her mother found this hard to believe and said, "My daughter is very timid and has not attended school yet. How can she become a talented general?" Even though the fortune-teller gave no answer, this prediction had an impact on little Shuxia and she made up her mind that she would make the dream of becoming a talented general come true somehow.

In the summer when Shuxia was eleven, it was very hot and her oldest sister's two small rabbits were dying from the heat. Her sister tried to get rid of the rabbits, but Shuxia took them back. She thought to herself, *They are two lives. How can I not cherish them?* Then, in secret, she raised the young rabbits and protected them from heat stroke. The two rabbits thrived and eventually had lots of babies that Shuxia fed wild grasses to. The babies thrived as well and Shuxia was able to sell them at the market for more than one hundred yuan each. This was a lot of money and with it she bought clothes for her parents and cotton cloth with which to make clothes for her brothers and sisters. There was just enough cloth for everyone else, but not any left for her. She didn't mind, though. She didn't care about making herself beautiful and it was enough to see the others happy.

That same year, Shuxia was picking corn in a field with some of her brothers and sisters and chatting with a neighboring villager called "Old Yao." Old Yao was talking about exchanging the good, strong corn stalks for coal after the autumn harvest to fuel their winter stove. Without thinking, Shuxia said, "So you want to exchange corn stalks for coal to have warmth in winter! I think you will have your final day tomorrow and it is better you protect yourself."

Her brothers and sisters looked at her aghast and burst out with comments like, "What the heck are you saying? Don't talk like that!"

Her parents heard about the incident later that night and her father said, "Old Yao is only about fifty and a lively man. How can you say such a thing?" But, once again, Shuxia did not back down. She said, "I see Old Yao as a stiff corpse, not a lively person."

The next day, as Old Yao was eating breakfast, he suddenly slumped over and never stood up again. Finally, people began to believe Shuxia's predictions because everything she said always came true.

The Surprising Satchel

Shuxia did not understand her own innate talents, especially as more and more unusual things started happening. For instance, when she was allowed to attend primary school, something occurred that shocked everyone, including her. Because her family was so poor, she did not have enough money to buy paper to write on. She used to collect paper that other students had already written upon and had discarded so she could write on the blank back sides. Sometimes she would use the stationery other students had playfully folded up and thrown around as paper airplanes. And the pen Shuxia used was the tip of a real pen attached in a makeshift way to a sorghum stalk.

When Shuxia looked at the other students' pretty stationery, pens and pencils in abundant quantities, she couldn't help thinking, *If only I had those, it would be a wonderful thing that would help me study a lot.*

This was nothing more than an innocent fantasy and she was very surprised when her teacher later made the announcement that, "Some students have lost their supplies and there may be someone in the class who is stealing." The teacher then asked each student to reveal the contents of their satchels in front of the class, one by one. When Shuxia emptied out the contents of her own satchel, everything the other students had lost came pouring out! She had no idea what to say or how to explain it.

"Please believe me—I did *not* steal these things, and I don't know how they got into my satchel!" Shuxia pleaded.

Later, more events happened of a similar nature in school, and the teacher finally realized that Zhang Shuxia had psychokinetic abilities and it was these rather than any malicious intent on her part that caused these things to happen. Her own subconscious extrasensory powers somehow simply caused things she wanted to jump into her satchel!

This same phenomenon sometimes got her into trouble at home with her own siblings. But for the most part, she got along well with her seven brothers and sisters. The only exception was her oldest brother. For some reason, he was very cruel to her. One time, she took two eggs from home without permission and traded them for two notebooks and two pencils for her schoolwork. Somehow her brother found out, and he started to beat her with a hard plastic pipe for taking the two eggs. She ran from his blows and pushed her head into the opening of the cold wood-burning stove in their kitchen to protect her head and face. Her brother continued to batter her body viciously until she became unconscious. Shuxia's mother tried to stop him, but she couldn't. Then he threw a bucket of water on Shuxia to wake her up.

Shuxia never understood why this one brother of hers hated her so much.

Chapter 2

Entering Society

When Shuxia finished elementary school, she was sent to live with one of her older brothers and his wife for three years in order to be homeschooled and receive the equivalent of a high school education. But this education came with a price. While she was twelve, thirteen, and fourteen years old, Shuxia was forced to work tirelessly for her brother and his wife as a servant in their home. It was a very hard time, and she was often treated *worse* than a servant. So, when she turned fifteen, she hoped her hard times were over and that she could finally go out into society and find odd jobs to do.

Within a year, Shuxia was finally able to get work at a highway construction site with other villagers, where all the workers lived near the site and slept in tents. It was the first time she had experienced this sort of collective living, and it felt wonderful to her. She thought, *This is what a normal life is like.* The job also provided a decent income for her to give back to her family. At sixteen, Shuxia began to feel that everything was going well for her at last. Little did she know her new life was about to change.

One day, while walking to the communal dining hall at the worksite, Shuxia felt a strange sense of uneasiness come over her and started to lose self-control. Suddenly, she fainted on the road. Her companions were stunned and could not understand how this strong, healthy young woman could lose consciousness so quickly for no apparent reason. The head of the worksite came over and yelled, "Hurry—take her to the hospital!"

Strangely, Shuxia had instantly gone into a deep coma, and none of the doctors at the hospital could figure out why.

The Other Side of Coma

For seven days without eating or drinking, Shuxia lay in a coma in the hospital bed. The only thing that kept her from being regarded as dead was that the doctors could still detect a very, very feeble breath. All the hospital staff could do, however, was to watch her and wait.

What those around her did *not* know was that, while Shuxia's body was in a deep coma, her spirit had gone to a place that was out of this world—a place where strange people welcomed her! Among them was an elderly man with a white beard and white mustache, who said, "What took you so long?" Then he said, "Don't you know us?" Shuxia was very surprised at first and tried to recognize the people greeting her. It seemed that she knew them, but not exactly. She did not know what to say to them. The elderly man with white hair seemed to be a high divine being of some sort. He led her to a residence and told her, "You can stay here. Tomorrow you will start practicing your divine powers."

"What are these powers I will be practicing?" she asked.

"You already know," the old man said. "They are the *Chinese Divine Powers*. How can you forget them?"

Shuxia was in that other-worldly place for a full seven days while hospital workers observed her and waited for her to come out of the coma. She later recalled that she practiced the whole set of Chinese Divine Powers during the coma. At the end of the seven days, the old white-haired man came to her and gave her a push.

"Out you go!" he said, and she started to wake up in the hospital bed.

Feeling very heavy and confused, she heard someone shouting, "Zhang Shuxia's eyes are moving!" as she opened her eyes.

Though she was now awake, all was *not* well. Everything had changed. In fact, Shuxia was totally different after she emerged from the coma and was no longer able to behave like a normal person. Her eyes would often just stare at nothing, her mouth would mutter strange things, and sometimes she would walk outside in the day or night without any idea of where she was going.

People said, "She's gone mad," and, "What a nice girl. How can she be so mentally disordered?" Shuxia knew they said these things because she could hear and understand them. But she could not understand what was happening to her and could not do anything about it. She could not change her outside behavior, and on the inside, she was different. On the one hand, people around her were thinking she had gone mad. On the other hand, she knew that, during her seven-day coma, she had gone to another place and had learned all sorts of strange things. Reality was different for her now.

For a long time, Shuxia continued having difficulty focusing her thoughts. She could not think clearly and was considered a lunatic. Because she was not in her right mind, she could not work. She needed someone to take care of her and had suddenly become a burden to her family. In the winter of that year, when no one was paying attention, she slipped out and went to her older brother's house in Lanzhou City. But when her brother and his wife discovered she had lost her mental stability, they were very worried about her and, for the sake of her safety, sent her back home by train.

Later, Shuxia could not remember how she even got to her brother's home or how she later went to her uncle's house in Lingyuan. Her uncle sent her back to her parents as well. It was December 23rd of the Chinese lunar year when she arrived at her parents' house. Her first year of being an adult and stepping out into society had been a disaster.

Shuxia did not want to be a burden to her parents and eventually wandered off again, not knowing what she was doing or where she was going. She found a cave and decided to live there. She had no supplies and only rags to wear. Her thinking was foggy, but she was somehow able to figure out that she could get enough free food and water from a nearby temple to barely sustain herself. For nearly two years, from about age sixteen to age eighteen, she lived in this cave by herself. During this time, Kuan Yin, the Bodhisattva of Mercy and Compassion, visited her every night as she was falling asleep. While she was half awake, Kuan Yin taught her the Buddhist sutras, or scriptures. Shuxia could see her in a white gown with her hair pinned back in a special way.

Eventually, Shuxia left the cave and wandered off again, once more with no idea of where she was going. Somehow, she traveled hundreds of miles. She had no money, not even a single coin. She was still out of her mind and did not know what she was doing as she crossed over fields and through villages and towns. She did not know how far she'd gone and had no idea as to what kind of food or drink she'd had or how she'd gotten it.

One day, Shuxia's mind cleared just enough for her to realize she was sitting in the railway station of an unfamiliar town amidst a noisy crowd of people. She heard someone say the railway station's name was "Saertu," which was in Daching City, about two thousand li from her home! (The traditional distance of a li has varied a little in China over time, but the modern-day li is considered to be about a half kilometer, or approximately one-third of a mile.) So, she had somehow traveled nearly 700 miles.

Being a little more clear-headed at this point, Shuxia found a bench to sit on and suddenly became aware that she was very hungry. After rummaging through her pockets, though, she realized she had no money to buy food or drink. All she had was a crumpled-up handkerchief. She looked at her hands, touched her face and body, and realized she had become so thin she was practically skin and bones. She looked around and saw other people wearing overcoats, and some even wearing fur because of the cold weather. Yet, she had on just a thin, shabby cotton jacket.

Shuxia was only eighteen years old and a stranger in a strange land. She wanted to cry but had no tears. Her mind was still not fully clear, and all she could do was look at her shadow, lament her lot, and wait for the arrival of her "Lucky God," as an old Chinese proverb says.

A Vision and Rescue

What Shuxia did *not* know at the time was that a very special old woman, who was a Buddhist nun and healer, lived not far from there and was coming to get her. The day before, the blessed Kuan Yin had come to the old nun in a dream and told her there was a girl in a nearby village who needed her help. Kuan Yin then showed the nun what Shuxia looked like and where she would be, and instructed her to go find this girl, take her in, and teach her.

So, as young Shuxia was sitting in the railway station of the strange town, hungry, dirty, and not knowing what to do, she suddenly heard someone whisper in her ear, "*The Goddess of Mercy asked me in a dream to pick up one disciple here, but I do not know who I am meeting with right now.*"

Shuxia looked up and saw the compassionate face of a thin, old woman dressed in Buddhist attire. Suddenly, her heart started beating faster. She felt like she had finally found a beloved family member and savior. She was astonished and happy all at the same time!

The nun tapped her on her head and Shuxia's mind immediately felt more clear. With kindness in her eyes, the old woman gently asked, "Girl, where do you come from and where are you going?"

"My home is in Kezu," she answered shyly. "I don't know how I got here, and without any relatives or friends, I don't know where I shall go."

Shuxia started to cry, stood up, and threw herself into the old woman's arms. The kind old nun wiped her tears away and said, "Kezu is more than one thousand li from here. Since you have come by yourself, won't your family members worry about you?"

Shuxia answered with humility, "I am ill and don't know how I came here."

The old woman replied, "Follow me, and you shall keep me company. I am old and lonely. And we all know that *if there is a bond between them, two people will meet across a thousand li.*"

Entering Society

Shuxia found out later that when the nun first saw her in the railway station, she had seen divine halos around Shuxia's body and guardian angels protecting her.

When they got to the old nun's home, Shuxia saw that it was worn and simple with little furniture. She lived a poor, austere life. But miraculously, upon arriving, Shuxia's mind suddenly cleared up completely and she felt healthy once more. All her muddled thinking, perplexity and confusion were gone in an instant along with any physical ailments she had been feeling. It was quite a while before she found out that this nun was a healer of extremely high cultivation and skill. Simply being in the nun's presence and in the domain of her residence—which was a paranormal environment in itself—could dispel all the poisonous elements from Shuxia's body and mind, and allow the wisdom and goodness that was natural to her to come back. Thus, her intelligence, inspiration, powers of understanding, and wisdom all returned quickly. And these all came back with an extra measure of quality and strength!

Young Shuxia was so grateful that she knelt down before the old woman and asked her to be her teacher.

"As I know you to be kind and sincere, I agree to your request," the old woman answered affectionately. "Please stand up."

So the gentle, elderly nun became Shuxia's teacher and master, and a whole new phase of Shuxia's life began.

Chapter 3
Training Commences

Now Shuxia had a permanent, peaceful place to live and, with the kind-hearted nun as her mentor, life was much better. She also had a skill to learn and the promise of a future. As a disciple, she was able to closely observe her teacher and learn the art of healing firsthand. Shuxia's own innate talents were so strong already that she could learn much just by watching her teacher at work. After all, she could already see inside people's bodies, an ability she'd had since she was a child. Since her master's reputation was so formidable and she was known far and wide as an effective healer, there were always many people coming to her for help. The old nun set broken bones and cured all types of traumas and illnesses. She used herbal treatments as well as energy and spiritual healing. She had very advanced medical skill, yet was always kind, quiet, and humble in appearance. She was also a vegetarian.

Meditation and Hand Stamps

For the first six months, Shuxia would cook three meals a day for the nun and all the people who came for healing. Then she would meditate with her teacher before falling asleep every night. She was given more and more spiritual practices over time to help her develop her own skills and soon was reciting Buddhist sutras every morning and practicing more advanced meditation. A sculpture of Kuan Yin was displayed only during times of prayer. At all other times, it was covered with a piece of painted paper. As a new disciple, Shuxia was given the Buddhist name "San Bao," along with four Buddhist items. These were: a "Catching-Demon Pestle," a "Nine-Dragon Ring," a "Divine Bell," and a "Medication Spoon."

Shuxia's master was impressed with her ability to understand and learn quickly. She taught Shuxia many things, explained the intricate, profound details of Buddhist concepts, and helped her to cultivate her own natural paranormal abilities. Once, her master explained that the purpose of the sitting meditation is "to forget everything . . . including yourself." She told Shuxia,

> In order to make you forget everything mortal and get rid of all your earthly normality, including your selfishness and individual desire, so that you can get the natural essences from the mountains, the rivers, the moon, and the sun, you should undertake a forty-nine-day-and-night sitting meditation.

Shuxia eventually did the sitting meditation continuously for longer than forty-nine days. During the meditation, she began to experience a most intriguing feeling and state of absent-mindedness. Then, she felt a white light penetrate her and her entire body became transparent, with the intestines, bones, muscles, and even the cells clearly visible. Shuxia felt as if she were sitting on a lotus flower, with her spirit clean and free and her mind clear and jubilant . . . a feeling of entering paradise on earth.

She discovered, however, that it is not easy to enter into Zen (or Chan) meditation. One has to give up all worries held inside, all thoughts of losses and gains, all affections and desires, *even all ideas*, to get to a realization of the free realm without memories, aspects, supports, or influences of any kind.

Shuxia's master taught her all about the body, its organs and systems, and how to set bones. She did not teach her the practice of acupuncture, but she did teach her how to open up key acupuncture points around the body for those who came to her for healing and how to infuse chi energy into those points. Shuxia's master also taught her how to make special patterns with her hands and fingers. The translation from Chinese for this practice is "Hand Stamps." Shuxia was told that these unusual hand poses functioned as *liaison signals* to higher masters in the spirit realm, but she didn't know at first what they were really used for. Finally, she learned how to use these unusual liaison signals to help her treat patients. Her teacher explained,

> The so-called 'hand-stamp' involves making different patterns with the fingers. It is a kind of liaison signal with higher masters, part of the creation of the *Mi*-section of Buddhism, and it contains the wonderful power coming from the universe. In general, to concentrate all the energy and spirit on the lower belly—the *dan tian* point—with palms facing upward is the basic cultivation form in Buddhism. In Taoism, it is called *liang dan*. Actually, both Buddhism

and Taoism are the same in concentrating the energy and spirit on one point so as to have the combination of Heaven and human beings. When the universe is me, then I am the universe, too. And once reaching this realm, the utmost divine powers of Buddhism are achieved.

Shuxia's master taught her how to concentrate this power or energy from the universe into certain parts of her own body and how to use it for healing.

Sleeping ABOVE the Bed

Shuxia's admiration for her teacher grew and grew. She learned that the old nun was originally from the Buddhist Pavilion of the Goddess of Mercy at Emei Mountain. Her Buddhist name was Zhen Xiu (pronounced "Shoo"). She had been married, but her husband had died, and now she lived by herself. Shuxia soon realized this kind and gentle woman had not only perfected the Buddhist sutras but actually possessed an extremely profound cultivation of them. One night, Shuxia awoke and got up to use the bathroom. As she was walking to the toilet, she saw that her master was asleep. But the nun was not lying on her bed, as Shuxia had expected. She was in a sitting posture *levitating more than a foot above her bed*. Shuxia was stunned and later found out that her master slept this way every night!

When Shuxia asked about her ability to levitate, she replied, "Oh, it's a sitting meditation, which is a high-quality skill in Buddhism." Shuxia found out that the old nun would start out meditating every night, sitting on her kang (a traditional Chinese sleeping platform).

The nun would eventually fall asleep during her meditation and, at some point during the night, her body would float upward and levitate . . . still in the sitting pose. Nothing supported her body or arms, however, an open umbrella with the handle removed had been suspended upside down above her bed so she would not float up so high that her head hit the ceiling.

There is an old Chinese saying that humbly decrees, "When I do good deeds, I do not ascend to Heaven, nor do I hurt the earth." Thus, suspended between the ceiling and the floor was the noblest place to be. Shuxia's master explained that all of her energy became centered during the meditation, and this would lift her up during the night. But she never explained this skill in detail, and Shuxia never learned how to do it herself.

First Attempt at Healing

One important aspect of the master's healing technique was to rid people of spirits that were attached to them or of negative spiritual karma caused by deeds from the past. This required an advanced level of psychic ability, but Shuxia was a natural at it since she'd had strong psychic abilities since childhood. Though she was still in training, an opportunity arose one day for her to try out her healing skills. It was a day when her master was very busy, with many patients waiting for her. Shuxia noticed that the head of the Bureau of Datong District had brought his blind wife in for treatment. His wife had been blind for more than twenty years. The nun was busy with many patients, so Shuxia offered to see the woman herself and use her own extrasensory skills to try to help the woman.

The official was hesitant at first and would have preferred to have his wife treated by the famous Buddhist nun, but he agreed. After examining his blind wife, young Shuxia said to the official,

> Your wife's disease has something to do with you. Thirty years ago, when you were fifteen years old, you crossed a narrow river ditch where you came across a small white snake with a red crown. You picked up a stone and hit the small white snake's head until it was dead. The residual information of death accompanied you back home. Actually, the revenge should have been upon you, but you had responsibility endowed by God to demolish the evils on Earth. So the revenge was transferred to your wife, who fell down from a high platform when she was twenty-five years old and lost her sight for more than twenty years.

Upon hearing what Shuxia said, the head of the Bureau was stunned. He admitted, "Yes, when I was a teenager, I did bash a white snake with a red crown to death with a stone, and I never told anyone about it. Not even my parents. How could you know?" He mumbled, "It's incredible, really incredible!"

When the head of the Bureau had first arrived at the clinic and saw Shuxia there, young and poor, he hadn't paid much attention to her. When she told him she would like to examine his wife, he had strong doubts. But as he listened to what Shuxia said, he was amazed and felt very ashamed. He repeatedly thanked her and said, "I know I have to apologize for what I have done. I promise I shall never kill any living thing again. I swear!"

Shuxia could tell the man was sincere in his remorse and felt compassion for his wife, who had suffered the loss of her sight for twenty years because of something he had done. So, with mercy in her heart, Shuxia waved her hand several times before the woman's eyes, directed several puffs of her breath at her eyelids, and recited some prayers. Suddenly, the woman blinked her eyes as if they had been touched.

"How many people are in the room?" Shuxia asked her. The woman looked around and answered, "Seven."

The head of the Bureau quickly counted the number of people in the room, and there were indeed seven. He hugged his wife and they cried together. Then the woman struggled free from his embrace and shouted, "Where is my savior? Where is my savior?" The head of the Bureau took off his hat and, holding his wife's hand, knelt down in front of young Shuxia.

Shuxia's first attempt at healing had been a huge success! She was so excited that she proclaimed, "One shall not only love one's own life but all other lives as well!"

Over time, Shuxia's master observed that she had worked hard and had gained a very good understanding of Buddhism. She wanted to elevate Shuxia's training to the next level and teach her even more profound mysteries. But to do so, Shuxia would have to take "tonsure," which is a Buddhist ceremony performed as part of the initiation of a novice into the first level of being a monk or nun. It always involves shaving of the head and not marrying. Shuxia was not yet prepared for this and still longed to marry and live a somewhat normal life. So she stammered out excuses to her teacher about her family situation. Her wise mentor could tell she was not yet free from human desires and passions, so the matter was dropped.

Even though Shuxia declined to take tonsure, she still continued to be a faithful disciple. She lived with her kind and loving teacher for about two years, learning her special art of healing. When she was finally ready to leave the safe, healing atmosphere of her mentor, her beloved master said to her just before she departed,

> My good disciple, you must not mention my name, but you have to enhance Buddhism. You should keep up the Buddhist mind, save the common people and cure the sick. Only through kindness will you gain the fruits and proper consequences of a dedicated life in this world. Keep this in your mind always. Don't try to please the public. You will go through a lot of suffering, and only by the accumulation of good deeds can you receive enormous merits and virtues. You might set up your own school and make contributions to society. Now you can go.

With that, Shuxia departed with her four Buddhist items and headed back to her hometown. She never forgot the words of her master. She went back to her family and once again entered into society, continuing her healing work as much as she could. Later, in 1991, when she was twenty-nine years old, she was able to use money she'd saved up from her healing work to build a new house for her kind master at the foot of Phoenix Mountain near Chaoyang Cave, to give her a better home and place for further practice of her charitable healing work.

Over the years, Master Zhang went back to visit her beloved teacher many times. This gentle, kind, and wise old woman had tirelessly helped untold numbers of people in need, and had trained numerous disciples before she passed away in 2012 at the respectable age of 103.

Chapter 4

Struggling to Be a Healer

Marriage

SHUXIA WAS ONCE AGAIN in the village of her childhood. She'd been away from home, studying with her master, for about two years. Soon after she came back, and on the urging of her parents, she got married. It was an arranged marriage, as was the custom in those days, so her new husband was not of her own choosing. In fact, her parents had arranged this match before she was even born, while she was still in her mother's womb.

Shuxia had a lot of domestic duties to do as a young wife, but she did not forget what she had learned from her master and continued to help people with her healing skills whenever she could. In the beginning, most of her patients were relatives or friends, whom she felt she could not say "No" to. But the story of how she had cured the Bureau official's blind wife had spread and she soon found herself sought after by many sick people who needed help. After more and more people recovered and her reputation grew,

Shuxia became widely recognized as a powerful healer who could cure a variety of illnesses.

It was natural for the villagers to come to Shuxia for healing and she was always kind-hearted with them and enjoyed being helpful. But her new family—the family of her husband—did not appreciate her special abilities. They wanted her to focus on her domestic duties, and her attempts to offer healing or any other displays of psychic ability caused great tension in her home. However, Shuxia could not turn away all the people who needed help and she also felt an obligation to use the Chinese Divine Powers she'd been taught.

One day, in June of 1984, during a meal, Shuxia inexplicably put down her chopsticks and closed her eyes. She was acting strangely and her new family members didn't understand what she was doing by suddenly becoming quiet and closing her eyes at the table. They worried the mental trouble she had suffered after her coma might be back. Shuxia then suddenly opened her eyes and said in a panic, "My mind has received information that tomorrow at noon there will be a natural catastrophe!"

Her husband's family now *really* worried that her illness was back, and they became nervous and angry at her at the same time. "What is this catastrophe? Don't say such nonsense! Who will believe you?"

"Aren't you all afraid to die?" Shuxia asked.

"What do you mean, *die*? Don't talk crazy," her husband chided.

At that point, everyone realized Shuxia was speaking clearly and behaving normally, and, therefore, she was not mentally unstable. But they continued to argue against what she was saying.

"If there is to be a disaster, how can we escape from it?" they asked. "And, if we can escape from it, then it would not be a disaster!"

With this reasoning, they didn't pay any more attention to her and ignored her warning completely.

Tornado

The next day around noon, while lunch was being prepared, there was loud shouting outside the house and Shuxia hurried outside to see what was going on. She looked in the direction other villagers were staring and saw a gigantic yellow and black atmospheric front quickly moving in from the northwest. Suddenly, someone shouted, "Look! Two big fireballs!" Shuxia could see two large twisted tornadoes that looked like huge dragons with golden horns—one yellow and one gray—baring fangs and brandishing claws. The twisters were dashing out from the airflow and rapidly rolling down upon the village!

Almost instantly, one of the tornadoes hit Shuxia's house hard. Doors and windows cracked and then the whole back wall of the house fell down! Shuxia involuntarily fell onto her back, as if pushed by something, and then was pulled up into the sky together with the roof of the house! As she was battered by wind and sand, she lost consciousness.

When she finally woke up, she found herself yet again in a hospital, confused again, like when she woke up from the coma. She was later told the tornado had pulled her up more than ten meters high and that she had then fallen back down into the house only to be buried in sand and stone up to her neck. But the most critical thing that had happened to her was that, during this ordeal, an iron nail had been driven right into her head by the tornado!

The nail had pierced deep into Shuxia's brain through the baihui point at the top of her head. (The baihui point is a very important acupuncture point at the center and top of the skull.) But, amazingly, she suffered no damage to her brain at all because the nail had entered in the best possible way, perfectly inserted and angled straight down between the two hemispheres of her brain. The nail was easily removed by doctors and, amazingly, after being raised up high in the air, falling down, being buried in sand and rubble, and having a nail driven into her head, Shuxia suffered only minor scratches over her body and was easily able to recover.

Other parts of the village suffered some damage—with two houses and parts of three others destroyed, a large date tree split down the middle, and a pig and a cow killed—but no other people were seriously hurt. Luckily, Shuxia's young daughter remained unharmed, though she had been buried in sand and stones. Also, Shuxia's thirty chickens were all intact. Overall, the rest of the village was relatively unharmed compared to the damage that had been done to Shuxia's house. In some ways, it seemed as if the tornado had been aimed at her home!

Actually, as much as nine days earlier, Shuxia had psychically foreseen that a catastrophe would happen. She just had not known *when* it would occur. It was a day when some people from a nearby village had come to her, imploring her to cure a boy with leukemia. The boy's mother had begged Shuxia, lamenting that they had been to numerous hospitals, but all in vain. They were always told his disease was incurable. The mother said, "Please help us. He is a good boy, and I am a school teacher with many students relying on me."

Shuxia's heart was touched and she declared, "The boy should not die." Then, she started using her divine powers to find the

Struggling to Be a Healer

extrasensory information she needed. The information she retrieved showed her the boy was on the list for death, and she understood that if she chose to save his life, she herself would have to suffer a catastrophe as compensation. But Shuxia had made up her mind to cure the boy and could not go back on her word to the mother. So she treated the boy, knowing there would be consequences. After nine days, the boy's leukemia was cured. The day his disease was cured, June 9th, was the day the tornado hit Shuxia's home and drove the nail into her head.

Details of the tornado incident were presented in the Kezu County newspaper dated June 16, 1984 and the *Chaoyang Daily* dated June 20, 1984.

Afterward, some of the villagers started saying things like,

> 'After surviving such a great disaster, you are bound to have good fortune in later years,' and, 'Zhang Shuxia is a good person, and she did not die—even when she was buried in the sand and stones during the tornado catastrophe—because the gods protect her. So she only got some minor injuries.' And, 'She not only is not seriously hurt but also has profound divine powers to cure diseases. Maybe she is an incarnation of a Buddhist god!'

What was interesting to Shuxia, however, was that, after returning home from the hospital, she discovered that a new paranormal phenomenon was beginning to happen. A kind of screen would appear in her mind every once in a while that would display extrasensory information on it. At first, things on the screen looked somewhat vague. But gradually they became clearer and clearer. At the same time, whenever she used her x-ray vision, the inside of people's bodies became even more clear than before. Later, she even developed the divine powers of remote (distant) extrasensory investigation and micro-description (seeing things on the microscopic level.) She eventually came to believe the nail impalement had actually *enhanced* her paranormal abilities, possibly by somehow opening up the circulation or other pathways of energy in her brain.

Soon, the news of curing the boy with leukemia spread all the way from Kezu to Linyuan, and everyone started saying that incurable patients should seek out Zhang Shuxia. Thus, she had an ever-increasing number of people to heal every day.

Most who came to her were poor, but Shuxia always had sympathy for them and helped them even if they could not pay. Though she was often tired from working day and night, her husband's family did not like what she was doing and not one of them supported her. At first, they were worried about her. But later, they outright opposed her healing work because it interfered with her getting her household chores done. They scolded Shuxia and tried to stop her from healing people in every way they could.

On the other hand, the villagers praised her as a good and kindhearted person who helped people, often free of charge, and whose treatment was generally accurate and effective. Those who came to her for healing started calling her "Master Zhang," and because her patients kept having good results from her treatments, she gradually became famous. Sometimes, people burned incense sticks and papers in front of her and called her a goddess, or they showed their respect by kneeling and bowing down so low before her that they touched their foreheads to the ground. Shuxia found this awkward and embarrassing. It was not what she wanted or asked for. And, unfortunately, this type of worshipping behavior fueled the irritation and dissatisfaction her husband's family was already feeling.

Then, there was a case that made an even bigger impact on Shuxia's life than curing the boy with leukemia. This time it was an eighteen-year-old boy who had run away from home because of his parents' arguing. His mother and father were desperate to find him and had consulted numerous psychics to try to find their son. Unfortunately, all the psychics they consulted told the parents he was already dead. But they did not want to believe it. Finally, they came to Shuxia for help. She focused on the boy and was able to psychically find out where he was. She told the parents their son was alive and that he was 200 miles away.

The mother suspiciously asked, "Are you trying to comfort me?" Shuxia replied, "No. He is alive and in three days will return to you at 10:30 a.m."

The boy *did* come back exactly when Shuxia said he would. At first, the mother thought she was seeing an illusion. She'd been so disheartened. But she soon realized he was real and was back home. The news of this boy's return and Shuxia's prediction spread fast, and people started worshipping her even more than before.

Unfortunately, those in charge in the local government had a negative reaction to the events and the worshipping behavior. Without cause, and under the influence of the non-spiritual communistic state, they arrested her and labeled her a witch, calling her spiritual/energy healings nothing but superstition. They even required her to walk around with a sign hanging around her neck that said, "Witch." Shuxia was embarrassed and humiliated, and felt cast out with nowhere to go.

Eventually, the authorities and her husband's family felt they needed to teach poor Shuxia an even stronger lesson. So, one day, they called a public security team which, along with her mother-in-law, brother-in-law, and some others, came as a group to confront Shuxia. They yelled at her and beat her up, shouting, "Beat her to death . . . let the Death Lord come to her!" Her brother-in-law yelled, "Monsters and demons, hell to you!" One of them even climbed up on the house, shouting, "Beat her! Beat her! We've never seen such a daughter-in-law!"

It was horrible. They broke Shuxia's left leg and inflicted terrible wounds all over her body. After the beating, they locked her in her room and no one was allowed to see her or bring her food or medical help. Only when she was near death and they were pressured by the public was she finally taken to the hospital for treatment.

The Lady in Blue

While in the hospital, many villagers from Shuxia's home town came to see her, and that was a great comfort to her. Another comfort was that, during her recovery, a wonderful lady came to her in her dreams every night. Shuxia called her the "Lady in Blue" because she was dressed in blue and had a bun-type hair style. She always smiled at Shuxia in these dreams and enigmatically said,

> Without regret, the mayfly will be born at dawn and die at dusk. And until seventy years old, one should know deficiency. It is because they all have been limited in a narrow space. Only through the unrestricted void can one understand life—even through one piece of flower, grass or stone. This is the way to transform the waste into magic.

Shuxia did not understand what the Lady in Blue meant by saying this, but when she tried to ask her more in the dream, the lady did not answer. She seemed to want Shuxia to figure it out for herself. Then she vanished. But the dream recurred several times, with the same message.

While continuing to recover from the brutal beating she had endured, Shuxia lay on her hospital bed and thought about what the Lady in Blue had told her. She also thought carefully about her own life and whether she had done anything wrong. She figured the only thing she had done was try to help people with her treatments. She did not cheat or swindle anyone, and it was not her wish for people to burn incense sticks or papers. They did that of their own accord. She cured illnesses and concluded that that's what she *should* do. So, Shuxia felt at ease and confidently decided she was doing the right thing. After leaving the hospital, she chose to continue her healing work, even against the wishes of her in-laws.

Pills From the Buddha

Finally, another event occurred that once again had a huge impact on Shuxia's life. In fact, it changed everything!

A teenager named Liu Cailian was brought to Shuxia for help. Cailian was the daughter of one of Shuxia's hometown villagers and was about thirteen years old. She had missed almost a full year of school because of debilitating headaches, and whenever she experienced these headaches, she would hit her head against the wall. Though Cailian had been taken to numerous major hospitals for treatment, the doctors could not help her. So, Cailian's mother brought her to Shuxia as a last resort and begged for help. Shuxia felt sympathy for the girl and could not refuse.

In her desperation, Cailian's mother asked Shuxia to request a remedy from the Buddha for her daughter. Other people who were present also very much wanted the girl to get well and joined in, hoping the Buddha would intervene. The mother pleaded, "Please ask the Buddhist god to send some medicine."

Asking for such a thing was something Shuxia had never thought of before, but she decided to try it. So, she folded a piece of white paper in front of her Buddhist altar and requested some form of medicine. She did not realize until later that, while she'd been in the hospital, the Lady in Blue had increased her paranormal abilities. The mother and daughter's pure feelings and sincerity also seemed to naturally enhance her powers at that moment. With everyone in the room watching, a large date-sized violet-colored pill dropped from the mirror of the cupboard right onto the white paper! At the same time, the room was immediately permeated with the fragrant smell of Chinese herbs.

Everyone was filled with awe and joy, especially Cailian, her mother, and Shuxia. Then, Shuxia heard a voice say,

> Not only will the girl get better, but she is going to help others through education.

No one else heard the voice but Shuxia. And the prediction it gave came true. After taking the divine Chinese medicine that had materialized as a beautiful violet pill the size of a large date, young Cailian's illness was cured and she was able to go back to school. She graduated from middle school and later from college and became a teacher. She finally became a Director of Education. Over her lifetime, Cailian taught many, many students, and a large number of them went on to study at Beijing's top university.

Shuxia hoped that, somehow, this new development in her abilities would gain her more credibility, relieve her of her worries, and solve some of the problems she'd experienced because of her work.

Chapter 5
The Year Without Sun

—⚏—

Shuxia was able to continue receiving medicine from the Buddha that materialized onto paper, but this newly acquired ability did *not* relieve her of all her worries or solve her problems. In fact, it made things worse. The news spread very fast, and more and more people flocked to her for help, asking her to request the special herbal medicine for them. Unfortunately, the more her fame grew, the more she was attacked by the various authorities for practicing suspicious activities. She continued to be labeled a witch by some, and others accused her of swindling money or referred to her work as superstition. Poor Shuxia had to endure more arrests and more overall torment.

Into the River

With so much abuse, part of 1985 and into 1986 turned out to be her "Year Without Sun." Looking back, Master Zhang would later speak of this time in her life sadly and described an attempt to relieve herself from her suffering in the following way:

> The voice of the people is something to fear. I felt wronged and took everything to heart. One night, at about ten o'clock, I walked along the Dalinghe River. After sitting a while on the riverbank, I thought, *My kind heart and good deeds cannot be understood and accepted. So I have no other way out. I have to put an end to my life.* I jumped into the river to commit suicide. But one who should not die will be saved anyway. It seemed that someone had been sent to save me. Right then, a person came along the riverside and saw me trying to drown myself. Immediately, he jumped into the river and pulled me to the shore. He was a decent man of middle age, and he sent me home. Afterward, I found out that his name was Xin Shushan. He was a man who saw what was right and had the courage to do something about it. Later on, he was interviewed by a reporter and praised.
>
> This might sound like a fictional story, but it was actually a real turning point of life or death for me. I thought to myself, *Why should I die? I have done only good things, not bad things that let people down. I should believe in what I have done and should not be afraid of living.*
>
> I then became determined, and I encouraged myself to live. On the other hand, I also thought to myself, *Why was there always someone to help and protect me? Was it the white-mustached old man or the Lady in Blue? Who else might it be?*

Though she was determined to do her best and go on, troublesome events continued to occur in Shuxia's life, one after the other. Maybe it was like what one ancient Chinese scholar said:

> When the heavens render a great task to one, they put his heart in troubles, his muscles in pains, his stomach with hunger and thirst, his body in emptiness, and his deeds in a mess in order to increase his strength and knowledge.

Arrested Again

In 1986, the Chinese government started a campaign to wipe out pornography and prostitution. This expanded to other undesirable activities as well, such as any spiritual or psychic activities. But the authorities could not distinguish between people who were frauds and those who were real psychics. The frauds were referred to as witches who robbed people of their money and belongings. So, at the young age of twenty-four, Shuxia was arrested again. Somewhere there was a gong and a drum beating, and the security officers told Shuxia they were going to parade her through the streets of the town. Shuxia felt unbearably wronged but had no one to go to for help. She was angry, afraid, and trembling. Slowly, her soul began to drift off with the sound of the gong and drum.

"Pull out the witch!" Someone shouted.

"Hang a black board on her neck!" Another shouted.

Hearing these cries, the color drained from her face, and she fainted. A man who'd been one of those shouting saw her lose consciousness and he felt something was wrong. So he jumped over to feel her pulse and her breath, which had appeared to stop. He thought she was in serious danger and waved his hand to get someone to take her to the hospital. At the same time, he disbanded the group that was surrounding her on the street. He was afraid that his participation in the ruckus might end up being responsible for her death.

At the hospital, a doctor came in to give her an emergency injection, but he could not do it. Even though the doctor tried and tried, he couldn't get the needle to penetrate Shuxia's skin! Someone in the hospital said, "That's strange." The man who had been the shouter then came forward and said, "The doctor is an idiot!" and tried to give Shuxia the injection himself. He couldn't do it either and finally calmed down enough to ask the doctor why the needle wouldn't go into her skin.

"I don't know," the doctor replied, perplexed. "This is the first time I have ever experienced such a thing."

"Maybe something is wrong with the liquid medicine," the shouter said. But as he was saying that, Shuxia's eyes began to flutter and she woke up. Once she had fully opened her eyes, she sat up like an ordinary person, grabbed her clothes, wiped off the dust, got off the bed, and put her shoes on. Then, severely stressed by the event, gasping for breath and confused, she quickly left the hospital by herself.

Chapter 6

FIRE

—⚏—

After the ordeals of trying to drown herself in the river and then being arrested and publicly humiliated, Shuxia tried to recover. But she was still in an impossible situation. She was constantly besieged by people needing her help, while the authorities and others continued to accuse her of being a witch. And her husband and in-laws would beat her if she tried to do more healings, especially now that they knew she might shame them by getting arrested again. She tried to avoid the people outside her house who were waiting for help, often by staying inside as long as she could or returning as late at night as possible to the small apartment she, her husband and their two children lived in.

One day, a woman in her fifties knelt down and grabbed onto her legs, crying and begging Shuxia for help. The woman had brought her father with her, who was blind in both eyes. And one of the woman's own eyes was protruding. It was heartbreaking and, once again, Shuxia could not turn them away. She saw psychically that, a while back, the woman's mother had seen two snakes mating by the side of their house. The mother had been afraid and told the father, who came out of the house and cut the snakes in half. Not long after that, the woman's mother had gone blind and passed away. Soon after she passed away, the father lost *his* eyesight. Then, while worrying about her father, one of this woman's own eyes had started protruding. She had come with her father because she'd heard that Zhang Shuxia was especially good at healing eye problems.

Shuxia saw psychically that it was the killing of the snakes that had caused blindness and death to the woman's mother and blindness to her father. She told the woman and her father to go to the place where the two snakes had been killed. They were to pray and acknowledge that the father was in the wrong for what he did and to ask for forgiveness. She then had some medicine from the Buddha materialize onto a piece of paper for them. The woman and her father went home with hope to pray for forgiveness and take the medicine. Later, this same woman and her father came to see Shuxia again, and the father had already regained partial eyesight in one eye.

But Shuxia's husband and family found out she had helped the woman and her father and later that day, her mother-in-law and husband's four brothers held her down and beat her badly again.

At this point, Shuxia was still very young—only twenty-five years old. The pressure on her was immense with countless people wanting healings from her, yet her family and authorities threatening her not to help them. She was tired of all the severe beatings and was completely despondent about her future. Though she had two small children, the youngest an eight-month-old boy, she did not see how she could go on. So, two days after her husband's family had beaten her, when a county official came and asked her if she would heal him, she agreed. When he offered her payment, she asked for a small container of gasoline instead of money.

Unfortunately, Shuxia's mother-in-law told her husband she had done her healing work again that day, and he got very, very angry. He shoved Shuxia with his foot, knocking her to the ground. Then he kicked her and hit her repeatedly with a metal shovel. While this was happening, Shuxia saw a white light and a vision of about seven or eight people she'd known in her life who had passed away. They were all females in their spirit forms, including a few students of hers. They were wearing beautiful clothes and looked like goddesses. Laughing at Shuxia, they said to her, "Look at you, putting up with that when you could have this!"

A Net From Heaven

In complete despair, Shuxia went outside her house late that night, carrying the container of gasoline and some matches. She locked her two children inside the house and climbed up onto a stack of corncobs. At the top, she sat down and proceeded to pour gasoline all over herself from head to toe. Frightened and unsure at the last minute whether she should go through with this, she held an unlit match and hesitated. She felt remorse about planning to leave her children, and she was worried about how her mother-in-law would treat them once she was gone.

Shuxia wasn't sure what to do, but her hands were shaking so much the match struck accidentally and lit her on fire! *WHOOSH!* She went up like a burning torch with her whole body on fire. It was so painful, she immediately let out a dreadful scream. Villagers heard the frightful sound, saw the blaze, and ran to her. But there was nothing they could do to put out the fire quickly enough to save her. Their water came from wells with buckets and there were no hoses or other access to water at hand.

Then, Shuxia felt what she could only describe as a "net" of some kind descending upon her and over the stack of corncobs. Miraculously, as it came down, it completely put out the fire! No one could see the net—the villagers only saw the raging flames inexplicably go out. They rushed her to a hospital as quickly as they could in a truck that normally was used to transport trash to the local dump. At this point, all of Shuxia's clothing was either burned off or stuck to her seared skin, and she slipped into unconsciousness.

She woke up in a hospital to the painful action of hospital workers trying to remove the remnants of her clothing. Some of her skin was coming off with the pieces of fabric. She had IVs stuck in her feet because there wasn't enough skin on her hands or arms to insert the IVs into those places. Shuxia didn't cry, though, or even shed a tear. She just kept thinking, *Why am I still alive? . . . Why didn't I die?*

To make matters worse, Shuxia's family would not visit her. People were still going to her house, wanting healings, but her husband's family and even the neighbors told them she was dead. Finally, people found out she was in the hospital and they visited her there and gave her their kind support.

Nearly all of Shuxia's clothes had been burned away, and her body was burned extensively. The doctor diagnosed third-degree burns on her chest and second- and first-degree burns on the other parts of her body. Luckily, her hair and face had somehow remained unaffected by the fire. The doctor said she had to stay in the hospital for a while to be treated for her burns, and Shuxia was put in an inpatient ward where trauma and orthopedic cases were treated. There were two other patients in her room—one was a lady with a large boil on her body, and the other was a man whose toes had been fractured in an accident.

Unfortunately, the care at the hospital was not adequate for taking care of all the patients' daily needs. Because she had IVs in her feet, Shuxia could not walk herself to the bathroom and, if a nurse was not available when she needed a bedpan, she simply had to wet the bed. Someone would then eventually come and roll her on her side to change the sheets. This caused her to develop infections in her burned areas, where yellow pus would ooze out from her skin. As a result of these infections, poor Shuxia had to stay in the hospital for a full three months.

The Spirit Master Returns

The emotional support the villagers gave to Shuxia helped, but the heavens also supported her. Not only had the invisible "net" descended to put out the fire and save her life, but something else started happening the first night she was in the hospital. The room she was in was on the fourth floor, and it had two pairs of windows. All the windows were sealed shut. Nevertheless, at 9 p.m. one night, one of the windows opened up. What the other two patients in the room saw was the window seemingly opening up all on its own. But what Shuxia saw was a white-mustached man outside pushing the window open, then coming into her room and over to her bed! He carried a small porcelain bowl with some sort of healing balm in it and he used a chicken feather to dip into the balm and gently spread it over her burned skin.

One of the other patients immediately jumped up and closed the window, thinking the wind must have blown it open somehow. But then, four or five minutes later, the two surprised patients saw the window open *again* and quickly shut on its own. What Shuxia saw, however, was the white-mustached man going back out through the window!

Shuxia didn't really understand what was happening. It was as if she were dreaming, but she wasn't. This white-haired gentleman looked like the old man who had greeted her and talked to her while she was in the seven-day coma years before. But this time, he had different clothes on. He was dressed in a Taoist gown like the costume of a knight. He had the calm countenance and demeanor of a transcendent being and was glowing with health and vigor. The small alms bowl containing the healing balm emitted a sweet aroma, and when he coated Shuxia's skin with it, he also poured out a bit of white powder from a small porcelain bottle and applied it to her wounds. All of this felt extremely cool and refreshing.

Before he left that first night, the old man told Shuxia, "You have a master on Earth, and I am your master as well. You can call me 'Master.' I will come to you at nine o'clock every night." She heard all this clearly and called him Master from then on.

When Shuxia awoke the next morning, her burned skin felt better. Then, at the end of the day, she saw the white-mustached old man arrive again. It was exactly 9 p.m., as he said it would be, and he was hovering outside the fourth-floor window of her hospital room once more. She watched him open the window with his right hand and enter the ward.

The white-mustached Master went to Shuxia lying in her bed and applied the medicine to her wounds as he had the night before.

FIRE

Then, without saying anything, he went back out through the window. The whole process was very quick, and the two other patients in the ward could not see him. All they saw was the window opening by itself, Shuxia acting like she was looking at someone, and shortly thereafter the window closing by itself. Shuxia's roommates were noticeably alarmed by this, so she tried to minimize their attention to what was happening by staying in her bed and not saying anything. But the other two patients inevitably got into an excited discussion.

"It is quite baffling that the window opens automatically!" one said. "There is no wind outside or in the room."

"How can the window open by itself? It's weird."

The woman with the boil blurted out, "My heart beat rapidly when I saw the window opening up. I shivered and got goosebumps. I feel ghastly and afraid in this room."

"There must be demons and spirits. I need a room change," the man with the fractured toes exclaimed.

Their complaints were relayed to the hospital management and a group of doctors and nurses, including the deputy director of the hospital, came to Shuxia's ward room to try to figure out what was going on. When they heard what the patients described, they didn't believe it, but they thought they should investigate that evening to see for themselves what was happening.

So, at about half past eight that evening, a group of people headed up by the deputy director of the hospital came to the enigmatic fourth-floor room. They sat and waited silently. When the clock on the wall struck nine, everyone stared at the windows. Right on time, a window opened by itself. Shuxia saw the Master come in and she said "Hello" to him. Everyone wondered who she was talking to. The Master quickly applied the medicine on her wounds and left the room. With a "Peng" sound, the window closed shut, seemingly by itself. Everyone looked at each other with blank stares. Some of them walked out of the room speechless.

The deputy director tried to smooth things over by saying, "Maybe it's the wind blowing open the window. Let's take a break, everyone." Then he left the room without further comment. The head of the hospital said, "We don't believe there are any ghosts in here." But he couldn't explain the phenomenon, and the other two patients were demanding to be moved to another room. There were no available empty rooms in the hospital, however, so these patients were simply moved in their beds out into the hallway.

More Divine Powers

After the other patients were gone and Shuxia was left alone in the ward room, the white-mustached Master came to her in a dream that night. She greeted him, saying, "Master, Master—please sit down." The old man said to her, "This time, I have come not only to cure your wounds, but also to teach you more skill."

"Master, what skill?"

"You have forgotten. It's a pity. It's a marvelous and wonderful skill for you to review, and you're going to take it not only to cure people, but also to deliver all living creatures from torment and to find suitable individuals to be your disciples." After waking up, Shuxia remembered what the Master had said to her in her dream. But, under the circumstances, how could she recruit disciples? *Maybe*, she thought to herself, *it means that I will be going into society again soon.*

The white-mustached Master continued to come back every night at 9 p.m. for nine nights in a row. He taught her four exercises of the

FIRE

Chinese Divine Powers. He was tough on her, too, and after teaching her something new, he would say, "My disciple, do you understand?" Sometimes she would answer, "I don't really understand." Then, he would say, "You're really stupid!" But he was only joking and would kindly show her again until she got it right.

While continuing to recuperate in the hospital, Shuxia stayed in contact with the Master in spirit in her dream state and learned the skills he taught her. In the process, she obtained a new divine power—the skill of sending Chinese medicine at a distance. Her powers had increased yet again. And the Master's treatment of her burns was so successful she barely showed any evidence of scarring afterward. She retained only a slight darkening of her skin here and there that no one could easily notice.

At one point, Shuxia's Master told her, "You don't have to heal people one by one. You don't have to request herbs for them. You don't have to bring all this trouble on yourself. All you have to do is tell people how to do certain exercises to help them heal themselves!"

While Shuxia was recovering in the hospital, she thought a lot about what her spirit Master had told her. She felt an awakening of sorts and thought, *Why should I suffer or die?* She decided she would do her best to stop giving individual healing sessions and find a way to teach people how to heal themselves instead, as he'd said.

Chapter 7

Finally Dead

But it was not easy for Shuxia to stop doing individual healing sessions. Too many people kept asking her for help. So, almost three years after her burn incident, when she was twenty-seven, she felt fortunate to have a new type of job opportunity present itself. It all started when Mrs. Li Shuqing from nearby Kezu County visited her. Her husband, Manager Che, ran a cotton and flax company in that county. Mrs. Li said that ever since she and her family had moved into their new home, her husband had been sick. He had developed a serious liver disease and she had also become ill. Their life had become uneasy and they quarreled, which was not normal for them. Mrs. Li invited Shuxia to visit her home and assess the house as well as her own illness. Shuxia had been interested in visiting that county anyway and agreed. Mrs. Li's husband, Mr. Che, was not at home at the time.

Strange Things

As soon as she arrived, Shuxia had a strange feeling that there was a bad omen of some sort or malevolent spirits affecting the house. Mrs. Li asked what could be done, and there were other people there wondering the same thing. Shuxia said that whatever was affecting the house simply needed to be removed and then everything would be alright. So she closed her eyes and started reciting prayers. Suddenly, "Peng! Peng!" was heard and, a few moments later, something dashed out of the house. One of the women saw it leave and screamed, covered her head, and ran out of the room. Then something came crashing down in a corner of the room with a loud bang.

Some of the people got up the courage to go over and look at what had come down. In one place, there was what looked like a thigh bone and in another, half of a human skull. As everyone stared in shock, Mr. Che arrived home. Shuxia explained that living in a residence with dead bones created bad airflow and that was why he and his wife had become sick.

Mr. Che said that if she could heal him of his liver condition, he would give her a job in his company. This could be great for Shuxia! At that time, it was very difficult for anyone living in a remote village to get a job in the city, and Shuxia was longing to leave her small town and hide herself in a new place. Now an opportunity was presenting itself that could make her dream come true. She felt if she could move to Kezu County and work in Mr. Che's company, she would no longer have to suffer the disharmony so painful in her life recently, with people wanting healing and her husband and in-laws not letting her do it. With the company job, she could stop doing individual healing sessions altogether and make a fresh start.

So, Shuxia used her x-ray psychic sight to look into Mr. Che's body. She told him he was in a late stage of liver ascites, a very dangerous condition if he did not get proper treatment. Upon Shuxia's request, three sacks of Chinese medicine materialized out of the air! Each sack had thirteen ingredients that were also written in strange and complicated Chinese characters on the bags. Shuxia herself actually could not read the characters. This type of manifestation in labeled bags had never happened before, but somehow she knew the medicine was to be boiled in water and taken seven times, while avoiding pungent and hot foods.

Manager Che was a man who usually insisted on scientific proof and was not easily convinced of things. However, after finding out about the strange things being expelled from his home, and after observing for himself that Shuxia could look into his body and make medicine appear in bags out of the air, he shouted, "Incredible, incredible!" So, Mr. Che followed her instructions and used the medicine. His health gradually recovered and the family became stable again.

A Name Change

Manager Che was so grateful and impressed with Shuxia, he offered her a job in his company as he had promised. She was bursting with joy and joined the County Cotton and Flax Company as a temporary worker. Her husband and children moved with her to Kezu County. In order to become as anonymous as she could and to avoid any further problems with the public, she changed her first name to "Ying." She was now officially "Master Zhang Ying," or more commonly, just *Master Zhang*. The name "Zhang Shuxia" was no more.

But, unfortunately, news of Master Zhang's involvement with Manager Che's wife and her dispelling of the strange things in Che's house quickly spread throughout the Cotton and Flax company and then throughout Kezu County. Once again, people who knew nothing about her or about what had really happened started to spread malicious gossip and untrue stories. This was very upsetting to Manager Che, but he was unable to do anything about it.

News of Manager Che's healing also spread quickly, and soon groups of believers started waiting at Master Zhang's place of residence to request help for themselves. Though she had hoped for a fresh start, life was once again becoming very difficult in this new county. She didn't mind working at the factory full time, but her salary was only 90 yuan a month. It cost about 20 yuan for a tiny, sparse apartment that she came home to, where she took care of her husband and two children. Her husband didn't work—all he did was drink tea, play Mahjong all day long, and wait for her to come home with money from her job at the factory. She often had to wait until the villagers hanging around her apartment left before she could go home. This put even more stress on her.

Eventually, the Public Security Bureau noticed all the people waiting outside the tiny apartment and started investigating Zhang Ying. For political reasons, because of her perceived superstitious activities, Manager Che was put under great pressure to let her go. As a result, in 1990, Master Zhang had to resign from the company.

Che and his wife, Li, felt extremely bad about this and worried about Master Zhang. They tried to comfort her and always expressed their gratitude for the help she gave them. Nevertheless, the impact of this type of unfair public treatment happening again weighed heavily upon Master Zhang. She had placed such high hopes on having a new and better life in Kezu County. Yet, once again, she was left wondering why she was always treated so harshly, like she was a bad person. And, once again, she began thinking death would be better than this life of constantly being misunderstood and mistreated.

After reluctantly resigning from the Cotton and Flax Company, Master Zhang went to a restaurant to eat a bowl of buckwheat noodles. Then, she went to a pharmacy and bought two packages of rat poison. When she got home, she poured the two packs of poison into her mouth and drank the contents down with water. She soon fell to the ground, lost consciousness, and began foaming at the mouth. At that moment, a jeep arrived at her house with a group of public security officers. This was quite ironic because the very government that had forced her out of her job was now coming to ask her if they could use her extrasensory perception to help them find some weapons that had disappeared. It was good timing, however, because she was quickly taken to the hospital and her family members were notified that she had tried to commit suicide.

This was Zhang Ying's third suicide attempt—the first was when she had tried to drown herself in the Dahlinge River, the second was when she poured gasoline all over herself and lit herself on fire, and the third was this drinking of rat poison.

Doctors and nurses at the hospital emergency center treated her very quickly and pumped her stomach. But she had taken such a large overdose of the poisonous powder that the damage was too serious and had already gone too far. As the clock ticked and hours passed, the doctors began to realize they were not going to be able to save her. With great regret, they finally told her husband that the family should prepare for her death.

Master Zhang died later that night.

THE DIVINE AND MASTER ZHANG

A death certificate was issued by the hospital and Master Zhang's parents, brothers, and sisters came and took her corpse back home. They had a coffin and burial clothes prepared for her. But her concerned father would not let them dress her in the burial clothes. He thought a proper explanation of why his daughter had died had not yet been given, and he wanted the people involved in her life, especially her mother-in-law's family, to clarify what had happened before going further with the funeral preparations. So her corpse was not put into the coffin right away and was left instead in a room in the house. Her lifeless body remained there for ten days on a funeral platform.

During that time, Master Zhang's spirit was standing in a corner of the house, watching everyone and everything that was happening, and hearing everything that was being discussed. On the second day, her spirit Master, the white-mustached old man, joined her in the corner of the room. He had an expression of reproach on his face and said to her,

> Only through terrible suffering and unbearable disaster can you achieve great and full understanding. You should *not* commit suicide! You should live and bravely enter into society to help the needy and relieve those in distress. After a while, your earthly Master will come to see you and you should go into society again.

Then, he vanished.

Master Zhang, in her spirit form, called after him, "Master, Master!" But he did not return.

Finally Dead

Her Earthly Master Arrives

The next morning, Master Zhang's earthly Master, the kind old nun, came to the house. She had received an urgent message sent to her by Ying's family, and she arrived with a young disciple named Xiao Fen and some other followers. When the old nun saw Master Zhang's corpse lying on the bed, she burst into tears. She then tried to comfort the family as people were hustling and bustling around. She presided over the redemption ceremony for the funeral and, along with her followers, stayed for several more days.

Finally, it was the ninth day after Master Zhang had been laid on the funeral platform and the end of the redemption ceremony. Her body was gray and starting to show signs of deterioration. Everyone was urging the family to put her body into the coffin as quickly as possible, but her beloved father still would not allow the burial.

"We shall wait one more day," he insisted.

At this late hour, the younger disciple, Xiao Fen, said to the old nun, "Master, I know that you can manifest divine medicine. Why not try to produce some for her?"

Hearing this, Master Zhang's elderly teacher was eager to do it. She exclaimed, "Alright—let's try!" (Buddhist masters with very high cultivation and divine powers are not supposed to bring someone back from the dead just because they want to. But if another person sincerely implores them to, that is a different matter. Then they may do it.)

So, the old nun closed her eyes and recited some prayers. After a while, she reached out over Master Zhang's face, and drops of red liquid medicine manifested out of the air and flowed from her hand into Ying's mouth. Soon, the corners of Ying's mouth started to change color. Her lips went from gray, to yellow, to white, and then finally to a healthy pink. Her body continued to change color from the head down. Once the effect of the medicine had spread to her chest, Ying's soul returned to her physical body and she moved a little.

"The corpse is moving! The corpse is moving!" one person yelled, running out of the room. Everyone else rushed in to see what had happened. What they saw was Zhang Ying waking up! The younger disciple, Xiao Fen, embraced Ying with tears in her eyes. The rest surrounded her and stared. All were stunned.

Someone exclaimed, "Incredible! How can a woman wake up after being dead for so many days? I've never seen such a thing in my life!" All sorts of comments were made as Master Zhang was carried off the funeral platform and moved into another room.

As if in a trance, Master Zhang felt someone holding her up. Then, she started to vomit. A dark fluid, full of black and purple lumps, poured out of her as she wretched over and over again. The unbelievable had happened. She was alive again. Her family members knelt down before the humble, gentle nun and expressed their heartfelt gratitude.

That first day, Master Zhang was very weak and could only rest and take a little soup and gruel. But on the second day after coming back to life, she had enough strength to talk a little with her master. After lunch on the third day, they heard that a neighbor's wife had hanged herself after a quarrel with her husband. So, the coffin and the burial clothes originally prepared for Ying were given to that neighbor for his wife. The old nun, her disciples, and the other followers went back home.

Finally Dead

Master Zhang had been dead for more than ten days, and this experience gave her a thorough understanding of life and death. She remembered the white-mustached spirit Master's instruction that she should go into society to help save people from suffering and disasters and was determined to do so. She now had renewed resolve to overcome any future difficulties and bravely prepared herself to go back into society once more.

CHAPTER 8

Service Home for the Aged

—⚍—

*A*FTER HER PROLONGED death experience, Master Zhang renewed her efforts to help people, but in ways that would hopefully *not* get her into so much trouble. She was particularly passionate about providing support to the elderly. So, in October of 1991, she helped set up a "Service Home for the Aged," of which she was Director. Three to four thousand people came together from Kezu County and nearby areas for the opening ceremony. That was the day she felt she was finally accomplishing her pledge to go into society. In a short speech to the public, she announced,

> I have neither high education nor working experience in society because I am only a common village girl. If it were needed, I would willingly give my life for giving you medication treatment. But I am not qualified to be the Director. I think [though] maybe it is the will of Heaven. And everyone who comes to the world must have a designated task. Now I am endowed with psychic powers for

curing disease and the opportunity to serve people. So, let it be. I will do my best!

After a huge applause, she continued by expressing her gratitude to those who had sent donations to support the new Home. After more applause, Master Zhang talked about its mission and said,

> If there are elders, whether workers or professionals, whom no one will take care of, they can come here. The Home will carry on the Chinese tradition of respecting and taking care of the elderly and will let them live peacefully in their old age. This is the purpose of the Home.

Many of the old people in the crowd were moved to tears by her kindness and compassion. Later, she manifested medicine with a flowery fragrance. Everyone was amazed and filled with exultation. Soon, people came and went in an endless stream, and donations grew to a sum of 18,000 yuan (almost 3,000 dollars).

Setting up the Service Home for the Aged was like a large stone thrown into the water. It evoked waves of effect and reactions of all kinds that spread out in every direction. Each day, more than a hundred people came to the Home seeking Master Zhang's special medication treatment, which she was now able to administer in a protected environment, and the number of residents at the Home increased rapidly. People praised her and some said, "A goddess has arrived in Kezu County." Everyone marveled at how she could see into people's bodies, find out what was wrong with them, and make medicine materialize out of the air onto paper to help people. The activities at the Home caused quite a stir!

Service Home for the Aged

An Old Woman's Plight

But the Home was more than just a place to help individuals. It provided Master Zhang with opportunities to do good that had far-reaching effects. One such opportunity occurred when a group of men brought in an old woman with a broken leg and many bruises and cuts on her body. The men said she'd fallen down a hill, but no one knew who the old woman was or where she lived. Master Zhang was very busy that day with many people hoping to receive help from her. Nevertheless, she attended to the old woman immediately while the others waited their turn. She said to the men who'd carried the woman in, "It is a traumatic injury, and she should be sent to the hospital. Why did you bring her here?" They told her they'd already been to the hospital but because the woman had no money, the hospital wouldn't treat her.

"Where are her sons and daughters?" Master Zhang asked. But the men said they didn't know.

So, Master Zhang reset the woman's broken leg and attended to her other minor injuries. Then she had the woman assisted to a bed where she could sleep for a while. Master Zhang had to go back to helping the other people waiting for her, but at the end of the day, she was able to get back to the old woman. Finally, she was able to ask the woman who she was and where her family was. What came forth was a very sad story.

The old woman had become a widow at the age of twenty-seven and had suffered a very difficult life, raising two children on her own. Her main job was as a button-hole maker on jackets. There were usually about seven holes per jacket, and for this work she was paid the approximate equivalent of twelve cents per jacket. Even so, she worked so hard she was able to send both of her children to college. When she fell down the hill, she'd been on a mountainside with a stick, looking for dates she could pick. The pits of these dates were used as herbs and she could sell them for a little money. But after a misstep, she fell and rolled down the hill. Lying at the bottom of the hill with a broken leg, she called out, "Help me, help me!" hoping someone might hear her.

Luckily, a group of stone chippers who chipped stones for making cement came by. They heard her cries and were able to carry her to a nearby hospital. But no one knew who the old woman was. The hospital turned her away because she had no family members to sign papers for her, and she had no money to pay for her medical care. Another woman at the hospital immediately said, "Take her to the Home for the Aged. A woman named Zhang Ying charges very little to help people!"

So the stone chippers brought her to the Home.

Master Zhang still wanted to know more about the woman and hoped to contact her family. The old woman said her son had a very good job in the city and was the Party leader in a large factory. She reached her hand inside her shirt pocket to pull out a folded package. Inside three pieces of wrapped cloth were three coins (the equivalent of 3 dollars), along with her son's name and contact information.

Master Zhang remarked, "Your son doesn't treat you very well, so why would you want to leave him money?" The woman replied, "No, this is so if I die, someone can use these coins to call him, and he can come and bury me."

Then the story came out that this woman had lived with her son and his wife up until two years before. Ying asked the woman

Service Home for the Aged

why she was not still living with them. The woman told her that one day she had asked her son for a couple of dollars to buy incense for worshipping the Buddha, but her daughter-in-law would not give it to her, saying, "Why do you want two dollars to buy trash?"

The old woman continued, "I have my self-respect, so I left them."

But the old woman had no home or money to pay for lodging, and she wandered homeless for days. No one in her family cared enough to come looking for her. The woman said, "At night, I had to sleep under bridges or house eaves. If I had money, I went to temples."

Eventually, someone recognized her as the mother of a son who was an official and gave her the money to get back to her hometown. She first went to relatives. But after a couple of months, they said, "You have a son who is an official. Why should we support you?" So, the woman became a homeless person again and collected trash to sell for a little income. She also picked almonds from trees and sold the pits. The old woman lived this very meager life with no home, barely surviving for two years.

Master Zhang listened with tears but also felt her anger rising. "How can your son behave like this?" She got up and used the Home's telephone to call the number from the old woman's pocket. It was 10:00 at night, but she got through to a man and said, "Do you have a mother named . . . ?" He answered, "Yes, but she ran away and has been missing for two years."

Master Zhang told the son what had happened to his mother and that she was there with a broken leg. She said, "She misses you all very much. Can you come and visit her?" He answered, "Our factory is very busy and I cannot ask for leave."

At this point, Master Zhang wanted to slap him. She angrily lectured him: "How can you *not* take care of your mother, who has broken her leg? You ought to ask for leave to come here. Sons and daughters should take care of their parents. When you were young and sick, your mother always took care of you. Now she has broken her leg. How can you say you have no time? You have a mother who raised you in such a way so that you could become the official you are today. If you treat your mother like this, it is of no use for you to have sons and daughters. What you do to others will end up coming back upon you or your children!"

Then, the words coming out of her mouth next did not seem to be her own. She continued, "What if your sons were sick?"

He replied, "My sons are not sick."

She argued, "You are wrong. Your oldest son will have a high fever tonight and go into convulsions at 11 p.m. Then, your younger son will go into fever and convulsions as well." The official couldn't believe this. His two boys, aged seven and nine, were healthy and fine. Master Zhang said, "Believe it or not! My phone number is 65782. If your sons get sick, call me at seven in the morning."

The phone call ended abruptly and she was still very mad. The old woman heard what had been said to her son and became frightened. Master Zhang slept at the Home for the Aged that night, as she did on many other nights. At seven the next morning, the phone rang and Master Zhang said to the old woman, "Your son is calling." The woman said, "I don't think so."

But it was indeed the old woman's son, who haughtily said, "Who are you?" Master Zhang replied, "Who are you looking for?" He then asked if she had his mother and complained that his sons never got sick before, but now they were both sick and both had had convulsions overnight!

Service Home for the Aged

"Your mother broke her leg," Master Zhang admonished, "and you weren't even concerned! Your mother's illness cannot educate you, but your sons' illnesses can!" She then said sternly to the official, "If you want to see your mother, come within three days. If you don't arrive by then, I'll put her in permanent care here and you may not be able to see her at all."

After a day and a night, the woman's son, his wife, and their two boys arrived by car. He came into the Home very haughtily and pointed at his mother, saying, "If you want to come, come. But as soon as you wake up in the morning and open your eyes, just eat . . . don't talk."

Master Zhang slapped the man on both cheeks and told him to leave the Home. She would take care of his mother herself! She then scolded him, saying, "I asked you to *visit* your mother, not come and lecture her. I don't think I want to let her go with you." She then patted the two boys' heads and said, "Poor kids. Do you think they will get well with parents like this?"

The mother of the children desperately knelt down in front of the old woman, begging her to come home with them. She promised they would treat her well. But the old woman didn't show any response on her face until her son finally knelt down and said, "Mama, please come home." The two boys then knelt down as well and said, "Grandma, please come home with us. We have missed you." The grandmother started crying at this point, and the others began crying as well.

Master Zhang then said she would not charge for the woman's stay and that the man could take his mother home under three conditions:

1) The old woman was to keep in contact with Zhang Ying by phone.

2) The son and his wife were not to upset his mother anymore. They must treat her well.

3) Not only must they treat her well, but they should also care about other elderly people and do charity work.

Master Zhang then told the son, "Don't worry about your children. They are very healthy. They are also smarter than you and will go to very good universities and continue to be healthy. But if you upset your mother again, your children will have problems." She later claimed that these words, and much of the other things she said to this man, were not her own. Rather, she felt the words came *through* her from spirit. A Buddhist concept is that bad people get punished, and some higher force was coming through her to teach this lesson.

After a few months, Master Zhang called the old woman to ask her how she was doing. "Oh," the woman confessed, "I was living in hell before. Now I am in heaven. My daughter-in-law feeds me first and lets me watch over their money." She added, "They even treat the neighbors well!" And later on, Master Zhang heard that the woman's son had organized 2,000 employees at his offices to do charity work!

Master Zhang was pleased. By teaching this one person an important lesson of kindness and compassion, he then taught his family and 2,000 employees, and this then impacted *their* families, and so on. The two boys grew up healthy as Master Zhang said they would, and went to top universities in China. Master Zhang stayed in contact with the family for eight years, and they visited her again when the boys were in college. Later, when she lectured in their town, the family hosted her in their home.

Master Zhang subsequently said, "We preach in China very strongly that you must take care of your parents." But, even so, she never felt that what she said on that first night when she set the old woman's leg and later when her son came to get her, was from her. "After all," she says, "why would I want the children to become sick?" It would not be in her nature to threaten anyone with the health of their children. On the contrary, she believes it was the Buddha speaking through her and *his* words coming out of her mouth.

This case not only had a heart-warming ending to it for the old woman, but it was also a wonderful example of how, when just a few people change and start helping others, they can then influence countless more to change and do good deeds as well!

— OFFICIAL TESTING AND NEW POWERS —

Chapter 9

Testing Begins

—⚉—

THE SERVICE HOME for the Aged was a great success and continues to operate today. As usual, however, along with praise, rumors and slanders also developed and Master Zhang was again maliciously criticized. Many strange and absurd accusations were fabricated by those who simply could not accept how she did her healing work. However, for the first time in her life, she did *not* become bewildered or angered by these attacks. She'd been told by her white-mustached Master in spirit that the Home was not a place for her to stay long term and that she could not escape from hardship or suffering.

"You have to face difficulties with calmness," the Master had told her. So she remained patient and tolerant. But the county leaders were forced to hold meetings about the controversy surrounding her healing work at the Home. They decided the best way to solve the problem was to have some form of scientific testing done on her by an authoritative group to prove whether she was truly helping people with her paranormal powers or taking advantage of them by trickery. So they set up a special team to perform an investigation into her psychic abilities that would then report their results to the relevant government bodies.

By then, Master Zhang was about thirty years old and had been healing people and making herbal treatments from the Buddha materialize onto paper for years. Stories of what she could do had spread far and wide, and the Qigong Association of Kezu County became keenly interested in her. They wanted to be involved with the research team.

The I & R Team

In the second week of July 1991, a group calling themselves the *Investigation and Research Team on Zhang Ying's Psychic Powers* was formed (abbreviated as the "I & R" Team). It was headed by Gu Shixian, whose title was Deputy Director of the People's Congress of the County. Other team members were: Geng Weibang, Vice Chairman of the County Scientific Research Association; Jin Chuan, General Secretary of the Qigong Association; and Wu Fengshan, Chairman of the County Federation of Literature and Art.

The I & R team quickly organized how they were going to conduct the tests, and by the end of July, the first on-the-spot test was carried out in Jin Chuan's home, with eight men participating. Zhang Ying was asked to perform her x-ray vision and she did so on four of the men present, telling them what their individual health problems were. They each nodded in agreement. "Yes, you are right," they confirmed. Then, she proceeded to make medicine materialize out of the air, and each of the men received one thumb-sized pill that was rich in herbal aroma. Each pill was also a different color!

Testing Begins

Everyone was very impressed and agreed that Master Zhang had passed the first test.

Treating at a Distance

The team members decided the next test would be to see if she could *remotely* diagnose people and deliver medicine to a distant place. That night, the county leader, Yang Jiuzhi, waited beside his telephone for her remote x-ray vision diagnosis. Master Zhang remained at another house 5 li from Mr. Yang's house (approximately 2.5 kilometers). She made a long-distance psychic diagnosis of his internal health, which she explained to him over the phone. Other members of the team sat around her, observing. She told Mr. Yang that he had a shrunken cerebral defect and some other ailments, which she described one by one. He was very surprised and confirmed that the remote diagnosis was accurate. But he doubted he would receive any medicine because all the doors and windows of his house were shut.

After waiting a little, Mr. Yang reluctantly opened his front door and expectantly looked for a messenger to deliver his medicine to him. No messenger arrived, so he closed the door and went back to his room. When he entered the room, he smelled the fragrance of Chinese medicine and found a yellow date-sized pill on his table! He couldn't understand how it had gotten there, as no one had come into the house, and he anxiously went around, searching to see if anybody was there. He picked up the pill, examined it closely, and replied in a hurry over the phone, "I got the medicine!"

Master Zhang had passed the second test.

News of the county team carrying out tests on her reached Chaoyang City, where the prefecture was located. One day, the

THE DIVINE AND MASTER ZHANG

Mayor of Chaoyang City, Liu Xiangong, sent a letter to Master Zhang, asking her to cure his illnesses. She knew it was another test and went to his house. She performed her x-ray vision and correctly diagnosed Mayor Liu's health issues as well as his wife's. The mayor clapped his hands with appreciation and proclaimed that Zhang Ying indeed had psychic powers, that she should be protected, and should use her abilities as a healer.

Now that Master Zhang had passed three tests, her spirits were raised. Later, at about nine o'clock that night, she psychically received a message from the universe. The cryptic message was:

> Five dragons jump out from water for a visiting great person of outstanding virtue, waiting for this person to speak the truth, and Kemu shall become Gold Mountain.

Master Zhang never forgot this enigmatic message. But to this date, she still does not know what it means.

Zhang Ying was next asked to treat a young boy named Chen Qi, who was a very difficult case. When Chen Qi was three years old, he still could not stand or walk because of muscular atrophy of one of his legs. He'd been taken to many hospitals, but no medical professionals could give his parents any answers or help for the boy. When Ying first looked at Chen Qi, she knew exactly what his diagnosis was because she had already received information from the universe beforehand about the boy. She said to his grandfather,

> His illness is paramyotonia, but I can cure it. You need not worry too much. I can get medicine from the air and you can try it. If it works, then your grandson will be able to stand up within seven days and walk within nine days. If, at first,

the medicine does not work, then it is God's will that the illness not be cured. Then Zhang Ying added, *I know there is a possibility of curing your grandson's illness, because your whole family has done a lot of charitable deeds and accumulated merits that the heavens very much appreciate.*

The entire family listened and felt hope.

She then requested medicine from the Buddha onto paper and gave it to the boy. The next day, his grandfather told Master Zhang the boy was doing better. She went to his house and manifested medicine for him two more times that week. On the seventh day, Chen Qi could stand up for the first time in his life. On the ninth day, he could walk. The entire family was overjoyed, especially the boy's grandfather, who was particularly devoted to him. Chen Qi grew up to be a kind young man.

After this healing, Master Zhang's house became as crowded as a marketplace and the I & R Team was able to observe her perform a variety of other healings.

One interesting event occurred on July 28, 1992, when she was discussing some matters with the team members. They had gone to the house of a county staff member and Master Zhang felt something was wrong with the *qi chang* (energy flow of the site) in that house and the house next to it as well. After some scrutiny, she said to the members of the team, "The host of one house is sick, and the hostess of another house is sick, too, because there are *strange things* hidden in these two houses. Once the strange things have been gotten rid of, then the sick people will be alright."

Master Zhang then began her process of ridding the house of the strange things and a thundering noise was heard above as if something had fallen down. She looked up and said, "The strange thing has been taken away and it is now in front of the door." Everyone went outside and found a large hammer covered in mud lying on the ground.

The hostess of the house exclaimed with excitement, "Every night, I always hear a noise on the east wall like someone hammering a nail. I would get angry and blame the neighbor for disturbing the peace. One day, I could endure it no longer and visited the neighbor while it was happening. But their house was empty and there was nothing on the wall. I thought something must be wrong with my ears!"

Master Zhang took the hammer and looked at it. She told everyone, "The hammer was used by a construction worker who fell down from a scaffolding and was either killed or seriously hurt."

After removal of the "strange thing," the hostess of the house gradually recovered from her illness. She was very curious about the whole event and took the hammer to the construction company that had worked on the house. Someone at the company told her the worker who had fallen down was sent to the hospital and that this was the hammer he had used at the time. Master Zhang later explained that,

> Some people may not understand 'strange things,' and may think they are superstition. . . . It is not unusual to think this. But, actually, the strange things are things left behind improperly or with inappropriate disposal of location that cause damage to the natural surrounding environment. Those things will result in transmitting bad energy or information which will damage the qi chang. The people who live at that

Testing Begins

site will be affected with an imbalance in their body and will become sick if they do not have a strong immune system to resist the influence of the strange things.

On another occasion, Mayor Liu, whom Master Zhang had cured earlier, invited her to a business meeting with delegates from Hong Kong, Macao, and Taiwan. She accepted the invitation and went to the meeting even though her clothes weren't up to the style of the others. She thought, *Though I have no fashionable dress, it is alright because my psychic powers should display the talent of a village girl.*

At this international meeting, she diagnosed each person accurately and they were all amazed. Then, one of the attendees asked if she could cure his family members back in Hong Kong. It was the first time she had tried to perform a remote diagnosis at a distance of more than one thousand li, but she decided to try. Master Zhang immediately "saw" there were two people—a woman and a boy—and that the woman had been to many doctors to no avail. This was confirmed by the surprised businessman. She admitted, "I am not sure I can cure your wife's illness because it is a complicated and difficult one." But she was able to make a pill materialize that was the size of an apricot pit, and the delegate took it back home to his wife. After taking the medicine, his wife got well. Later, the couple made a special visit from Hong Kong to Ying's home to express their gratitude.

After more tests, all the members of the Investigation and Research Team were convinced that Zhang Ying's psychic abilities were real and that she was not a fraud. They wrote a one hundred-thousand-word report that officially concluded "Zhang Ying is in possession of paranormal psychic powers." The report was not an authoritative state document, but it did have a positive effect on Master Zhang's life at the time by serving as an effective counterattack to all the rumors and slanders that had been made against her.

Chapter 10

Going to Beijing

Ms. Zeng

THE LEADERS OF KEZU COUNTY now wanted to send Master Zhang to China's capital city, Beijing, to be tested by the very best scientists. It was set up that she would be appraised at the Human Body Research Institute of the National Defense Science Working Commission by a committee that included nine members, along with audio and video personnel.

One of the committee members, a woman named Ms. Zeng, was assigned to accompany Master Zhang to Beijing. Ms. Zeng was very doubtful about Master Zhang's abilities, had a smug attitude, and was full of confidence that she would have a chance to laugh at Zhang Ying in Beijing. She was the type of person who took pleasure in other people's misfortune and brought along a notebook to relentlessly record every event, one by one. On the way to the institute, she excitedly talked and laughed with the others in the group, but would not even glance at Zhang Ying.

When they arrived in Beijing, Ms. Zeng followed Master Zhang closely. She was to stay in the same hotel room with her and watch to make sure this supposedly psychic village girl did not carry out any trickery. She finally confronted her haughtily and said, "Zhang Ying, we are now in Beijing, not Kezu. This time, we have put great effort into carrying out an investigation of your powers, and it is not simple. If you cannot pass my own personal investigation, you are finished." Clearly, what she meant was that if Master Zhang could not see into Ms. Zeng's own body and describe *her* condition, then it was not necessary to go any further with the testing.

This was a direct challenge and Master Zhang could not help feeling the woman was a villain. She knew she did not have to answer Ms. Zeng, but she decided to calm down and, with neither a haughty nor a humble attitude, Ying spoke.

"Okay, please stand up. Let me see."

Ms. Zeng took her slippers off and stood up. Master Zhang merely had to glance at her for an instant before saying, "You have a weak liver and abnormal menstruation. You have taken a lot of different medicines, but they have not been effective. Your period has been late for three months."

Hearing this correct diagnosis, Ms. Zeng was astonished and blushed. Her self-satisfied attitude disappeared and she asked Master Zhang with humility, "Please tell me. Can my condition be cured?"

"Whether your condition can be cured or not depends on you. In daily life, stop stirring things up. Do more good deeds and charitable work. Be an honest person. When you look at things, you should seek truth from facts and not harm others to benefit yourself. Truly and whole-heartedly believe in psychic powers and do not force yourself to go against your own will. In this way, your illness can be reduced by half. As for the other half, I will try to make medicine materialize for you. If it appears, it is your fate. If I cannot do it, then there is no way out. Now wait."

Master Zhang was able to make a pill of herbal medicine appear for Ms. Zeng. She then said, "If you believe what I have said to you, you will get effective results in three days."

Ms. Zeng immediately changed her attitude and became friendly instead of critical. Master Zhang knew that Ms. Zeng was more or less a decent person with a sense that she had committed errors and was willing to correct them. So she took on a pleasant attitude toward her as well.

Controlled Conditions and Cameras

On the day after arriving in Beijing, Master Zhang was taken to the 507 Institute of China National Defense Science Working Commission. Several specialists and professors were on the team. The testing was to be carried out in front of video cameras and, to prepare Zhang Ying, two female assistants first helped her change all her clothes and put on only the clothes they provided her with. They then looked in her ears, nose, and hair to make sure she wasn't hiding anything on her body. After this, Master Zhang was permitted to enter the testing room and sit in a designated place to listen to their announcement of rules. During the test, she was not allowed to speak to anyone and no one could leave the room without permission. The test room was totally closed, with only a window connecting it to an outside room. Master Zhang felt a bit nervous in this sterile professional setting.

The first test was to see if she could detect shapes through a solid wall. Three types of sign boards—square, round, and angular—had been created and were sequentially displayed on the other side of the wall for a total of eighty times. Master Zhang was able to detect the shapes behind the wall with 70 percent accuracy. This was very disappointing to her, as she had expected closer to 100 percent. Even though 70 percent accuracy was much better than the average person could achieve and far better than chance, it was only average for the psychically talented person. The main examiner, however, explained that it normally takes at least three months of testing to truly establish someone's abilities and thus, she should not worry about this result.

But Master Zhang was still bothered. She wondered if the anxiety she was feeling in the test environment was affecting her, but she didn't really think it was that. Then she decided to calm herself and use her psychic powers to try to find out what was inhibiting her. As she was leaving the test room, a light flashed before her eyes and she suddenly knew what the problem was! She turned to the main examiner and exclaimed, "I know the reason why I did not have a good result in the test!"

The head of the team was excited and asked, "What is it? Speak up!"

"Between the seventh and eighth floor of this building, someone has put some ancient coins in the crevice of a window!" Master Zhang was implying that somebody was intentionally trying to cause interference behind her back, using their own powers against her in some way.

The entire examination team promptly went to the place between the floors that she had indicated and there were, indeed, three ancient coins shoved into the crevice as she had described. They were *cong ning tong bao* coins. Needless to say, the examiners were quite impressed with this impromptu display of ability. They also wondered, "Who is behind this trouble? It's too much to have such a trick occur!"

"I know who it is," Master Zhang proclaimed confidently.

"You know? How can you know?" they asked.

"I can make time go back and let the scene reappear," she explained.

"Well, then—speak up. Let's have it."

"He is a man of about forty, 1.7 meters high, with a bald head. His name has not appeared to me."

After thinking a moment, one of the team members said, "I know him. He is Mr. Wang of Peking University." Upon investigation, it was discovered that Mr. Wang did collect ancient coins and that he was skeptical of Master Zhang's abilities. He even admitted his trick was a type of magic he was exercising against her to trip her up and see if she was really psychic enough to figure it out. In other words, he admitted that he was testing her.

Three days later, the next official test was done, this time to test Master Zhang's ability to make medicine from the Buddha materialize out of the air. The Director of the Ministry of Health was there and, once again, two female military doctors helped her take all her clothes off, including her wristwatch. Then the female doctors washed her down. Master Zhang was again given a white lab outfit to wear, with no pockets and with sleeves that were snugly buttoned to her wrists. Finally, they led her into the test room, where a square had been drawn on the floor; she had to sit inside this square amidst video cameras and recorders. She started using her psychic powers, made her special request, and two dark red pills appeared on paper before her. The video cameras caught everything on film and all the supervising staff observed it. It had been recorded under rigorous scientific conditions and proven without a doubt!

Grabbing Medicine From the Air

Recording the appearance of the two red pills on film was momentous. But the next thing that happened was to prove even *more* momentous. One of the examiners said to her, "Since you can request the herbal medicine to appear on paper, why not have it appear in your hand?"

Master Zhang had never actually thought of this before. She only knew how to request the medicine from "all the Buddhas" to help a specific person, and then wait for it to appear on a napkin or other paper in front of her. But the phenomenon of manifesting medicine out of nothing is not unheard of in China and it is possible that the Beijing researchers already knew some of the history of this feat. In fact, there is an old Chinese phrase that describes it as "grabbing medicine from the air."

According to legend, in a matriarchal society that existed thousands of years ago, there was a goddess who was able to grab medicine from the air. Also, the family surname of "Zhang" is a long family line in China that is full of healers, and one of Master Zhang's ancestors was a healer at the Royal Palace. Many generations ago, there was a man in the Zhang family line who was a great healer and also "grabbed medicine from the air." Even as of this writing, there is a famous man still alive and living in China who can do this. His surname is "Zhang" as well, and his full name is Zhang Baosheng. So this may be why the researcher was bold in his question.

Master Zhang felt nervous about this request to have the medicine appear in her hand because she wasn't sure if she could do it. She was even worried that, if she couldn't accomplish this, then the researchers might think the accusations against her of being a charlatan were correct. Maybe they would arrest her! So, she anxiously thought about this the rest of the day. She wondered what she would need to do differently to make the medicine materialize in her hand as opposed to on a paper in front of her. She thought there *should* be a way, but she did not know what it would be. For just a moment that day, she saw a circle in her mind. But this made no sense to her.

The next morning, she was led into the same testing room again and made to sit in the same spot. This time, as she sat there, an image of two hands appeared in front of her face. The hands started to move and showed her hand postures and positions to make. One was a posture to make with her right hand and fingers, and one was a posture to make with her left hand and fingers. Then an image of how to bring the two hands together appeared. The vision was basically showing her to *do it like this*.

So Master Zhang mimicked these hand positions as she sat there in the testing room. Suddenly, three little herbal pills smaller than pine nuts appeared in the palm of her hand!

The head examiner looked at the medicine and said, "Is it possible to get a larger pill?"

Master Zhang felt nervous again. She knew how important this testing was to her own credibility, and she also felt she owed it to the people of Kezu County. So, she felt she must try. Time passed and the examiners waited. But nothing appeared. Finally, the leader said, "That's all for today." This was the last day of scheduled tests in Beijing, so there would be no more testing after this.

She thought, *How can it end this way? I might not have another chance in front of such a group of specialists to prove myself.* So she insisted they give her more time and allow her to try again. The leader agreed and announced they would allow her to attempt one more time. She did the hand postures once more. This time, a *huge* pill flew into her hands! It weighed 13 grams and was 2.6 cm in diameter. There was loud clapping and hearty congratulations on her success. Everyone had big smiles on their faces and Ms. Zeng was so excited she was crying!

In total, the scientific team in Beijing had tested her three times for manifesting medicine and she had succeeded each time. The official report of their scientific appraisal concluded that Master Zhang Ying was, indeed, endowed with psychic powers. One scientist, who was actually the first person to make an atomic bomb in China, wrote a glowing letter of acclaim that her abilities were "highly mysterious." And the panel of scientists gave her the title of "First Strange Mysterious Woman of the East." A letter written by the Beijing panel implied that Master Zhang was a National Treasure of China as well. However, this title was never *officially* given to her.

Though the scientific testing in Beijing had confirmed Master Zhang's unusual abilities, she was still bothered about achieving only 70 percent accuracy with her x-ray vision through the wall. Some of her supporters suggested she go to Shenyang to be tested at the Qigong Science Research Institute. So she went to Shenyang and was able to achieve very successful results there under strict testing. Everyone was so impressed that Master Zhang was invited to become a special member of the Liaoning Provincial Qigong Science Research Institute. She was given a certificate and was also invited to become a psychic researcher. After that, no one dared to criticize her in any way or to spread gossip about her!

Going to Beijing

Soon, Master Zhang received a message that General Zhang Zhenhuan, President of the Chinese Society of Somatic Science, wanted to meet her. This was big news and everyone was excited. She went back to Beijing and met General Zhang and some of his colleagues, including the head of the National Defense University. General Zhang put her through some informal tests of his own in front of everyone and she passed them perfectly. Clapping his hands, he said, "You are marvelous! It's psychic powers." He then took a photo of himself with her.

The General sent Master Zhang a letter afterward dated January 9, 1993, with an inscription in his own handwriting. He wrote:

> It has been confirmed by us that your psychic powers are really brilliant and rare, worthy of studying, and have to be supported and taken care of in order to create more conditions that will allow them to play an even more important role. I salute you!

This letter meant a lot to Master Zhang and her supporters. She received more and more invitations to various organizations but had to decline most of them. She could not forget her hometown elders, relatives, and friends. They needed her, and she needed them. However, now that she had official recognition from Beijing, she was invited to give many demonstrations, often in front of large audiences.

As Master Zhang performed more and more public demonstrations, her psychic, spiritual, and other paranormal abilities grew with almost no limit. And her new talents of being able to make pills manifest in her hand and powdered medicine fall down from between her fingers into others' hands were even *more* exciting phenomena than she'd been able to demonstrate before. A side effect from these new-found abilities, however, was that whenever she had medicine materialize in her hands, she would feel a sort of "electrical current" or shock that traveled from the base of her neck, through her right arm, and down to her right hand. This sensation is not painful, but she feels it every time. And, for some reason, after doing this probably thousands of times over the years now, it has caused her right hand to become a little bigger than her left.

Master Zhang at age forty-one.

With her mother, Du Lanrong, and her father, Zhang Benxue.

At a research center in Beijing, Master Zhang is surrounded by top government researchers who tested her paranormal abilities.

Giving an outdoor speech early in her career as a healer.

With members of a Chinese Naval Hospital who studied medicine Master Zhang manifested out of the air.

At a television filming studio, Master Zhang points to two herbal pills she manifested while on camera. One was for a woman with acute allergic rhinitis, and the other was for a boy with a congenital ear problem.

In the Chinese coastal city of Qin Huang Dao, Master Zhang explains our *limited* and *unlimited* nature to a packed audience.

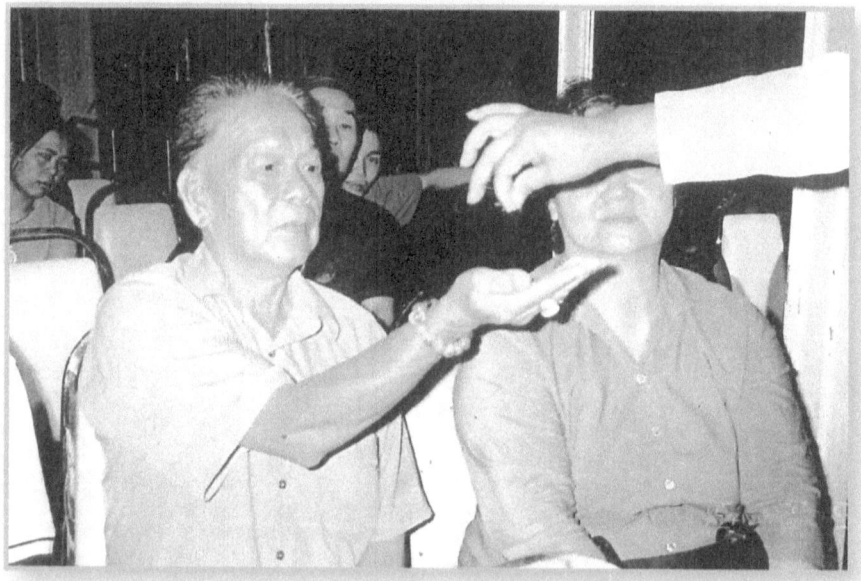

At a seminar, Master Zhang receives herbal powder from the Medicine Buddha for someone with high blood pressure, which she sifts between her fingers into his hand.

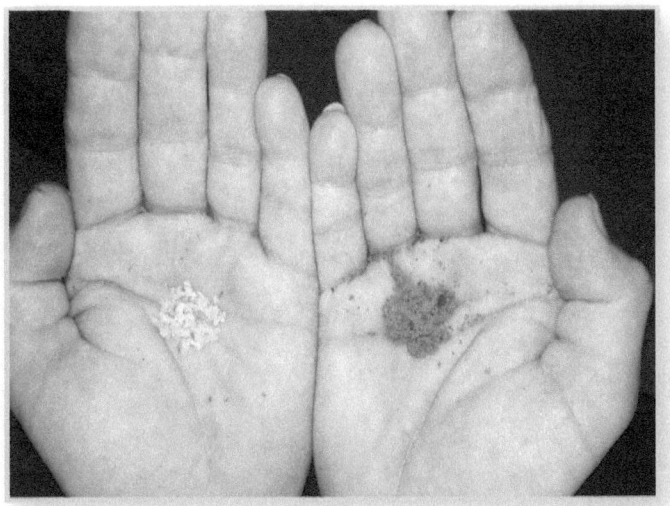

Herbal powders manifested out of the air into the author's hands. In this case, Master Zhang first sifted out the darker brown powder from between her thumb and first two fingers into the right hand. Then, she simply moved her hand about two inches and kept sifting powder without a break in effort; but into the left hand came a light beige powder.

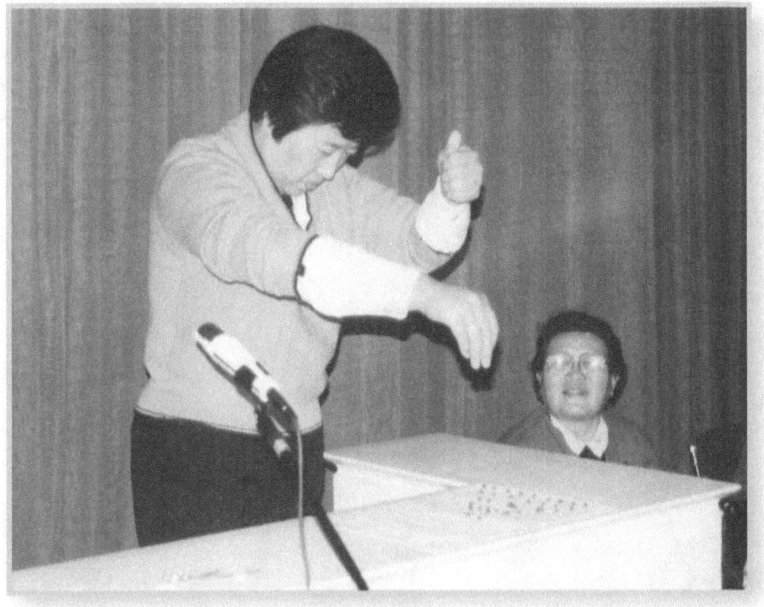

Producing small dark red pills, one after the other, from her hands at a lecture. Master Zhang produced more than 300 pills out of the air during this one event.

At a large event, participants put up their hands to receive energy Master Zhang is sending them. She can be seen standing in the crowd near the top of the photo.

A Mongolian man who had received healing from Master Zhang presents her with a traditional "hada" scarf as a sign of deep respect and appreciation.

Performing energy healing on an elderly woman in a wheelchair from the Hong Kong Bodhi Association who had a splintered type of bone fracture. Right after the treatment, she was able to stand up and walk.

A foreigner holds a glass bowl while Master Zhang proceeds to manifest liquid medicine from the air that drips down from her hands. Everyone is amazed.

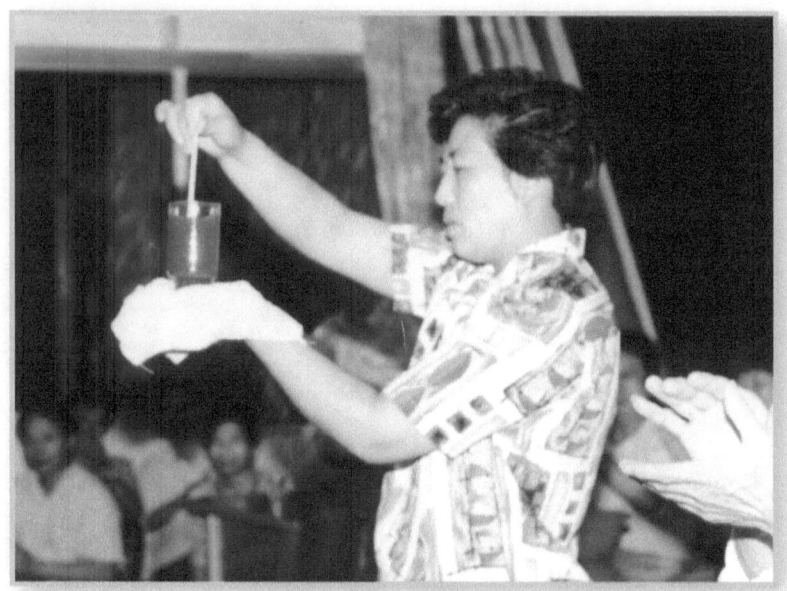

This originally empty glass was filled with liquid medicine that flowed from Master Zhang's hands. (A single chopstick is in the glass.)

At the Space Medico-Engineering Research Institute in Beijing, Master Zhang demonstrates how she transforms plain water into medicine water. Professor Kongzhi Song confirms its herbal aroma.

Master Zhang demonstrates how she first transforms plain hot water in some of these milk jugs into strong-smelling herbal medicine from the Medicine Buddha; then, changes those back into normal hot water and makes the other containers contain the aromatic medicine in them instead.

Four of these men are high-ranking generals in Canton, China. The man to Master Zhang's immediate right picked a common stone from outside and wrote his surname on it with a cross. Master Zhang then held the stone in her hand for one hour. At that point, it had turned into a golden nugget that was confirmed as solid gold by a jeweler. The man's surname and cross symbol were still on it.

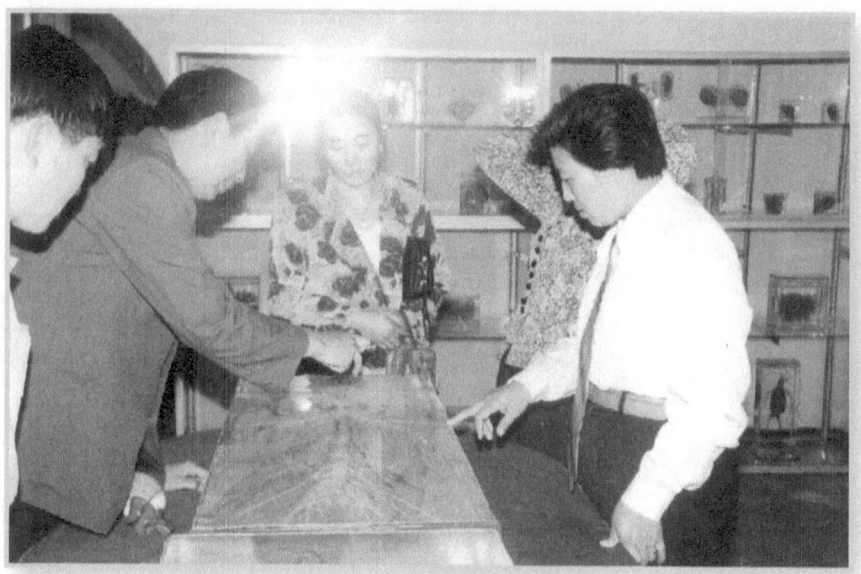

Master Zhang was hired to help archaeologists study mummies by psychically revealing aspects of how the deceased lived and died. Here she is dressed in white shirt and tie.

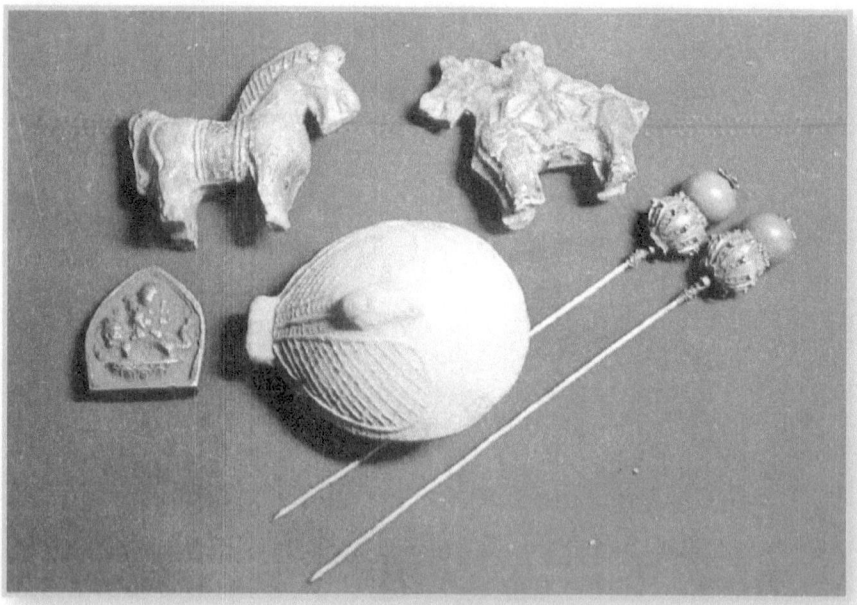

At one demonstration, Master Zhang manifested jade jewelry out of the air from the warring states of 475 to 221 B.C. Archaeologists pronounced them to be genuine.

On a visit to Tibet where she went to meditate and study.

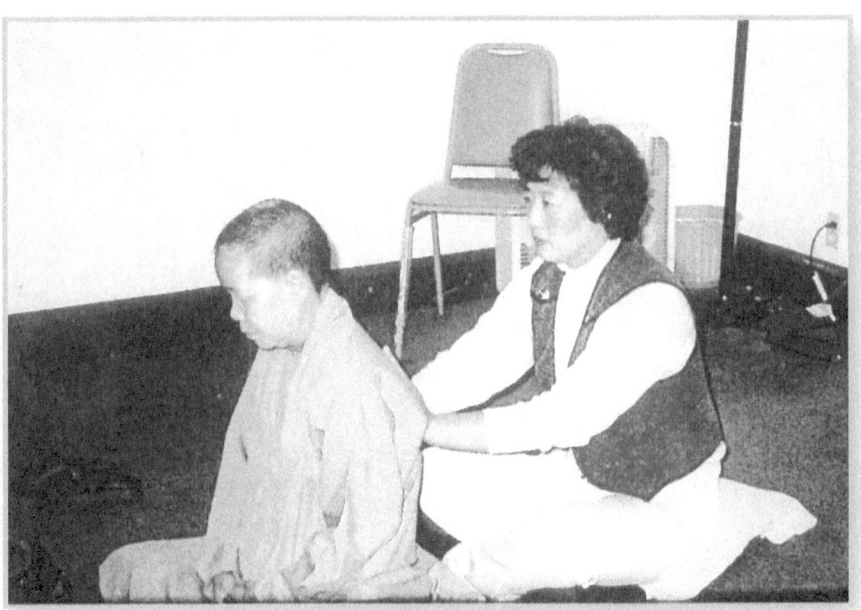

Performing energy healing on a Buddhist nun with lung cancer.

Demonstrating in Taiwan how to manifest liquid medicine.

With Mr. Shui Xia Xiong (on her left), consultant for the Japanese Central University and honorary professor from Toyo University in Japan.

Master Zhang (on far left) shopping with the wife of the President of Papua, New Guinea (in middle).

After the devastating 2008 earthquake in Sichuan Province, Master Zhang donated forty tons of rice. Here she is with Kim Holland, one of her primary interpreters in the U.S., and a long-time friend.

One of the classic paintings of Kuan Yin, the beloved Bodhisattva of compassion, riding a black dragon. This shows that black dragons are thought of as good in Chinese culture.

The image that suddenly appeared on a nearby tree in a flash of light after Master Zhang asked Kuan Yin in a park to show herself. Details can be seen that look like folds of a hooded robe and rosary-type beads hanging down.

A large golden manifestation.

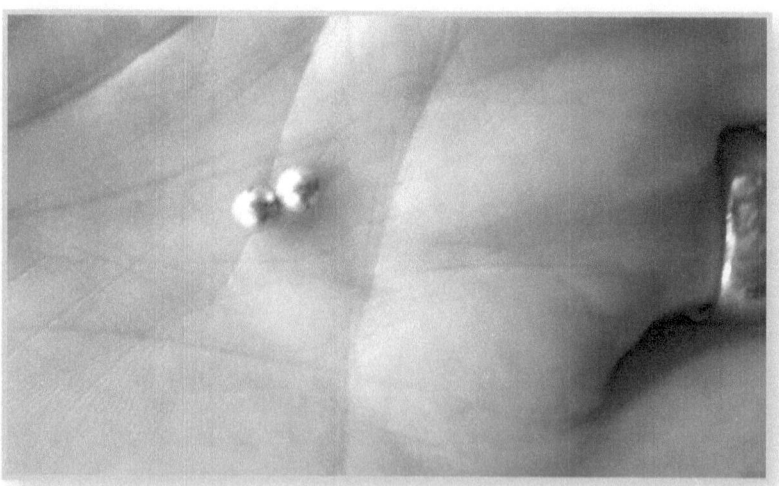

Two small golden manifestations.

Master Zhang holds up a large golden pill that she "grabbed from the air" as she stands in front of a poster of the Medicine Buddha who is holding up what looks like the same thing. He also has a bowl in his lap full of what appear to be more pills.

Front cover of one of the books published in China about Master Zhang, titled *Spiritual Light: A Collection of Cases Where Master Zhang Uses Her Special Abilities to Cure People.* Written by Jianxin Li and Qin Zheng and published in 1998 by Inner Mongolia Publishing Company.

Back cover of the same *Spiritual Light* book, showing two herbal manifestations in each hand.

Master Zhang was invited to give a demonstration at a celebration of the 10th Anniversary of Shanghai's *Economic Times* newspaper. A famous Chinese actress was asked to come up on stage to receive a manifestation from Master Zhang, who then caused a gold necklace and gold earrings to materialize out of the air. The actress later donated the items to a philanthropic cause.

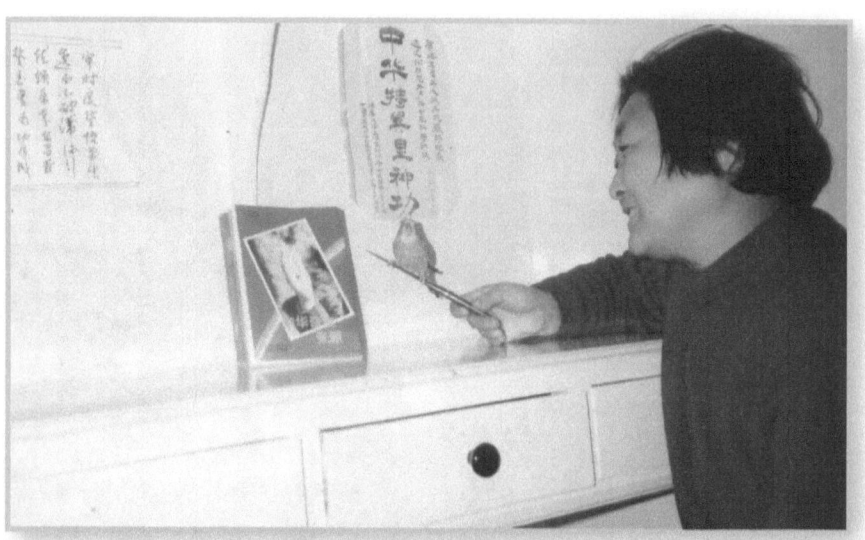

This woman's husband had late-stage stomach cancer. When he came to Master Zhang, four-fifths of his stomach had been removed and the cancer had already metastasized to his liver. He saw Master Zhang three times for healing sessions. Soon after that, Master Zhang was about to hold a large event at which she would lecture to five thousand people. The night before the event, the wife had a dream that two beautiful women came to visit her. The next day, when she attended the event with her husband, two parakeets enigmatically appeared and landed on her shoulders. After attending the event, her husband experienced a complete recovery and lived another fifteen years. Here, the wife is holding a bird in front of a book printed about Master Zhang. Note that the book cover displays a hand with a pill in it.

At the Chinese People's Liberation Army Navy General Hospital. The Dean of the hospital, pictured here with Master Zhang, was in charge of scientifically testing the healing effects of Master Zhang's manifestations on rats that had been injected with cancer cells. A controlled study was performed for ten days with half of the rats receiving manifestations and the other half not receiving them. The rats that did not receive the manifestations from Master Zhang all died within five days. Those that did receive it were still alive and very active after ten days. The hospital Dean drew a lotus plant for Master Zhang accompanied by words of praise and appreciation.

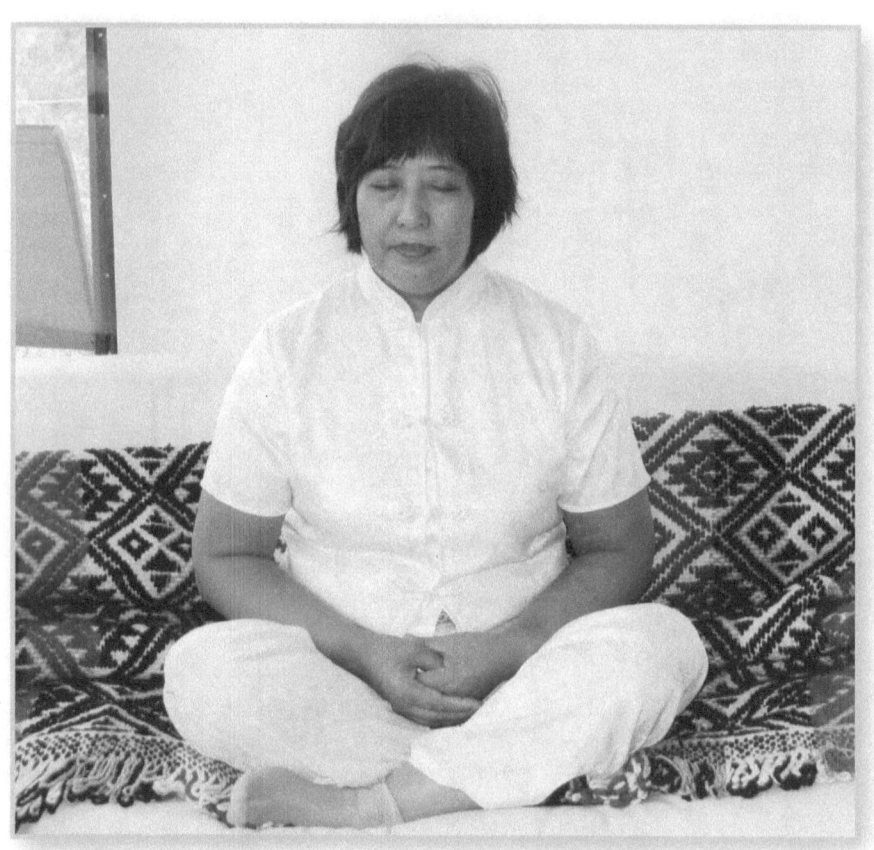

Master Zhang meditating.

Chapter 11
Raining Medicine

—ɯ—

The Ren Couple

*I*T WAS ALREADY KNOWN by now that Master Zhang sometimes received information about people *before* she met them. On one occasion, a man named Mr. Ren was convinced of her powers after watching her perform a demonstration and then personally getting a diagnosis from her. The next day, he brought his wife to see her. Zhang Ying was friendly to the man but not to his wife. Other people were also in the room, and they were all puzzled. Why was Master Zhang acting this way toward Mr. Ren's wife?

Suddenly, Master Zhang looked at the woman and said in an angry manner, "So you just have a tumor in your uterus?" She then stretched out her hand and opened it to show a black pill the size of a fingernail and handed it to Mr. Ren's wife. The woman was stunned and trembled with awe.

Master Zhang proclaimed, "Actually, I was not going to provide you with medication treatment. What have you been saying to your husband?" She then proceeded to tell Mrs. Ren, "You told your husband I was a swindler, a magician! You even said I had cheated him. You two argued for quite a long time and were still arguing even after you left your house. So, who is the real swindler?"

The woman's face first turned red and then white, and she could find no words to speak. So Master Zhang asked, "Did you do those things I am saying?" The couple nodded in amazement. Mr. Ren mustered up his courage and asked, "How could you know? Our home is far from here and my wife and I were the only ones there!"

With this, Master Zhang showed a small smile and explained, "It is my extrasensory perception. When I woke up this morning, I heard someone whisper in my ear, *After a while, there will be a couple coming to you asking for your medication treatment. You should not take care of the woman who doubted you.* The voice then continued to tell me the details I just told you. That is why I did not greet you with enthusiasm when you came to me." Master Zhang then added, "I am sorry for my rudeness." Everyone in the room laughed and the atmosphere relaxed. Later, Master Zhang heard that Ren's wife had completely changed her attitude and told everyone about Master Zhang in glowing terms.

Pill Within a Pill

The success of Master Zhang's testing in Beijing and official recognition by the general and others had a very positive effect on her life. Finally things had turned for the better, and the years 1993 and 1994 were particularly full of exciting events and demonstrations. For example, on April 17, 1993, Master Zhang was invited to demonstrate her skill to a gathering of more than sixty people, including provincial celebrities and qigong masters. Everyone anxiously awaited China's new "wonderful woman."

Zhang Ying began the demonstration with great success, correctly diagnosing a member of the group to a round of applause. Afterward, the host of the event asked everyone to calm down. He then said, "Please now let Master Zhang diagnose this old man, who has made great contributions in his qigong career." The old man the host was referring to was a distinguished, fully white-haired gentleman with a kind countenance. He rose out of his chair and bowed to her. She stood up and approached him with her hands clasped in the *heshi* Buddhist greeting gesture to return her heartfelt respect. (The heshi greeting is simply both hands pressed together in front of one's heart with the fingers pointing up toward the chin.) Then Master Zhang walked about two meters away and started looking into the old man's body and diagnosing him.

"You have dense blood fat. Your left eye has a small black dot that developed when you were hit as a child. You have a bit of arrhythmia. Your lung has calcifications, and your gall bladder has stones. Your pancreas is slightly red and both kidneys are weak. This shows you have the syndrome of diabetics. So you must pay attention to your head, heart, blood sugar, and urine sugar."

The audience was surprised once again with her detailed psychic diagnosis and proper use of medical terms. The old man was very happy and said with gratitude, "You are completely correct. I do have all the conditions you have diagnosed. The hospital gave me the same diagnosis last year. Thank you."

Without any difficulty, Master Zhang then manifested a green pill out of the air and said to the old man, "Though this pill is not large, it has been made with two different herbs. There is a small pill within it." Surprised, the old man split the green pill and found there was, indeed, another pill within it! He swallowed the pill and told everyone, "Yes. It's a pill within a pill made of two different herbs."

This caused another storm of applause. The host then announced to the audience, "Anyone who wants to be diagnosed by Master Zhang, please raise your hand." Of course, everyone in this gathering of celebrities and qigong masters raised their hand!

Liquid Medicine

Master Zhang thanked them for their trust but, with profound apologies, said she would only be able to examine a few participants that day. She thought about it for a few moments, however, and said, "Maybe we can do it this way. I can make up a pot of medicinal liquid for you. Would that be alright?" Everyone was very excited, especially when she realized one pot would certainly *not* be enough, so she manifested several pots of liquid medicine for them! When Master Zhang materializes liquid medicine from the air, it is usually a pink liquid that comes from her hands, though sometimes it is red. The audience had to collect it in whatever containers they had.

After this event, Master Zhang's reputation spread even faster. Manifesting liquid medicine was not a frequent thing for her to do and was to be reserved only for special circumstances. However, there were at least several other times that year when she produced liquid medicine and these events were observed by many. One was in November of 1993, when she was asked to give a presentation to the Liaoning Qigong Research Institute in the Henan Province.

Raining Medicine

On the second day of her presentation, more than a thousand people were there. Since she never had time to treat everyone, Master Zhang had begun the practice of giving out "Lucky Cards" to two or three members of the audience. These fortunate people would get an on-the-spot diagnosis and receive her medication treatment. On this date, one old man with rheumatoid arthritis, who was sitting in a wheelchair, received a Lucky Card. He was helped out of his wheelchair onto a chair on the stage. Master Zhang quickly told someone to get a bowl and she produced liquid medicine for him that flowed from her hands. Half the bowl was filled. A moment or two after drinking the liquid medicine, the old man felt pins and needles in his legs and had tingling and other strange sensations. She asked him to stand up. But the old man was so used to being confined to a wheelchair, he did not have a belt on to hold up his pants. So someone had to run quickly and get a rope to fasten around his waist to keep his pants from falling down. He then timidly raised himself up and stood.

"Please walk one step forward. Be brave. Don't be nervous," Master Zhang encouraged him. The old man wanted to lean on his walking stick, but she said, "Don't take the stick." With courage, he took one step, and then another and another. It was like a miracle, and the audience applauded wildly. Master Zhang later explained,

> Why did I make up liquid medicine in the air for the old man? It was because I got information from the universe that the old man always had done good deeds and kept good relations with people and Heaven. And his illness was quite severe, so that it should be cured by liquid medicine instead of pill or powder medicine, which has less effect. However,

to make up liquid medicine needs more psychic powers and is more difficult to do.

Miracle at the Pagoda

That same year, a truly remarkable event occurred with liquid medicine. The local Kezu County leaders sent Zhang Ying a special invitation to attend a ceremony and banquet held in honor of the twenty-fifth anniversary of the founding of her hometown in Kezu. At the banquet, many citizens and leaders were in attendance from surrounding counties. Some were able to receive medication treatments from Master Zhang. The audience repeatedly toasted and praised her and warmly appreciated what they called her *wonderful powers*.

After the banquet, there were performances and dancing, and Master Zhang decided to slip away from the festivities to visit a famous ancient Buddhist pagoda nearby. She was in a very good mood by the end of the evening and wanted to meditate at the base of the pagoda's magnificent statue of the Medicine Buddha to "interact with the individual intelligent spirit and strengthen her own powers endowed by the heavens." She felt it would enhance her ability to cure people's illnesses, and to serve society and the masses better.

Li Zhou's Ancient Pagoda is a cultural relic and protected by the province. It is thirty-one meters high (101.8 feet) and was built during the Liao Dynasty, which lasted from 907 to 1125 A.D. When Buddhists gather to worship at the pagoda at dawn, it is the grandest scene in Kezu. The early morning sun, graceful flying swallows, and beautiful landscape make this ritual look like an elegant Chinese painting.

Raining Medicine

But Master Zhang was not able to slip out of the banquet unnoticed. A few people saw her go and started to follow her. Soon, others joined. Eventually, there were about fifty or sixty people all walking to the pagoda along with her. The large group from the banquet arrived at the pagoda and looked up at the towering, serene statue with two old trees swaying near it in the moonlight. Everyone sat in a circle on the platform, and Master Zhang put her palms together, closed her eyes, and relaxed into meditation. All were silent. She entered a state of psychic powers and slowly opened her palms. Suddenly, there was a strong smell of Chinese herbal medicine accompanied by the sound of bustling leaves from one of the old trees. Then a slew of raindrops came down upon the visitors. Excitedly, everyone enjoyed the peaceful evening drizzle. After a moment, someone shouted, "These are not raindrops. It's raining Chinese liquid medicine! Master Zhang has sent us Chinese medicine in raindrops!" Everyone confirmed that's what they were experiencing and rejoiced.

It was quite a night. Finally, all the participants reluctantly left the pagoda with its tall statue and wise old trees, and went home. At about 11 p.m. Master Zhang herself fell fast asleep. Suddenly, an image of Bhaisajyaraja (the Medicine Buddha), sitting on his lotus pedestal, appeared in front of her. He was smiling and began dotting out two lines of writing very clearly for her to see. The words were:

> Practicing medicine in this world to promote justice;
> serving the people to broaden the prospective future.

Master Zhang never forgot those words from the Medicine Buddha or the experience of that very special night.

CHAPTER 12

International Recognition

—∞—

Huge Audiences

After receiving validation from the scientific testing in Beijing and recognition from group after group, Master Zhang had become quite famous. The public torment she'd endured through so much of her life was finally behind her. She began traveling a great deal and giving public lectures on the "Chinese Divine Powers" that her white-mustached Master in spirit had taught her. At these lectures, she often gave demonstrations of her healing techniques as well, but since she could not help every individual who wanted a healing, she continued to give out Lucky Cards in a random fashion to the audience. Those who drew a Lucky Card were able to come up on stage and be treated by her. Participants loved this, and more and more people attended Master Zhang's lectures.

At these public lectures, she not only demonstrated her x-ray vision and ability to manifest medicine out of the air but was also able to send healing energy (chi) to large numbers of people at once. This is an ability that highly skilled qigong masters generally have, so it is historically accepted in China. For instance, in one lecture, Master Zhang sent healing energy to an entire audience of 5,000 people!

Between 1991 and 1998, Master Zhang gave more than 400 public lectures. Over eight years, it was estimated that she lectured to between 300,000 and 400,000 people in approximately ten provinces of China, in more than forty cities, counties, and towns. She also lectured in Hong Kong, Japan, and other countries. The talented village girl from poor roots had certainly come a long way.

For a while after 1993, as can be seen in many of her photos, Master Zhang dressed in men's clothing and wore her hair like a man. This was because the types of things she was doing and the types of responsibilities she was taking on were not typical things women did in her culture. Her upbringing made it clear that a woman was *not* supposed to be seen outside the home or listened to on matters of importance. So, dressing like a man made her feel more confident. When asked if she believed that everyone really thought she was a man, she answered that she thought some did, and others did not know for sure. Looking back, Master Zhang later explained that she felt more powerful and free to do her work when she dressed like a man.

Girl with BB Bullet in Her Eye

Some especially interesting cases and events occurred in 1993 and 1994, which were particularly active lecture years. For instance, at a public lecture on November 20, 1993, Master Zhang was about to give her presentation on the Chinese Divine Powers in Zengzhou,

International Recognition

Henan (North Central China), where the venue was set to hold up to 8,500 people. Amazingly, more than 10,000 people swarmed into the huge auditorium!

The reason so many people were eager to attend her lecture that day was because word had spread quickly of something special that had happened the week before. Master Zhang had been invited to give a public lecture by the Henan People's Congress and the Provincial Qigong Association. At the event, an eight-year-old girl received a Lucky Card and, accompanied by her parents onto the stage, was able to receive an individual healing session.

In front of the large gathering, the mother tearfully explained that one of the girl's eyes had been injured while playing with her friends. An air gun had accidentally gone off and a BB bullet was accidentally shot into the girl's eye. Unfortunately, the doctors said it was impossible to do surgery because an operation would be too risky. The girl looked on silently and Master Zhang said to her, "Poor girl. What a pity to have such a pretty girl with one eye. Is it painful?"

"The swelling is painful and I am always in tears," the little girl answered. Master Zhang looked at her eye and said, "I will try to take the bullet out. Is that okay?"

"Yes, please!" the little girl answered.

Thousands of eyes in the audience were staring at the stage, waiting to see how the bullet was going to be removed, and all was silent. After a moment or so of concentrated attention, Master Zhang raised her right hand and pointed a finger at the girl's injured eye. At the same time, she said some prayers and started her psychic powers. One minute, two minutes, three minutes passed, and everyone in the audience was holding their breath. Those sitting near the stage could see that the little girl was perspiring heavily, with huge drops of sweat sliding down her face. Master Zhang's face was also hot and her right hand was extended as if she were about to pull something out of the girl's eye. Suddenly, she said to the girl's family, "Quick—bring a bowl!"

Immediately, the girl's father was able to grab a teacup and everyone heard the sound *"clink, clink"* as the air-gun bullet dropped down into the cup. Instantly, the entire audience was applauding and shouting! The girl and her mother knelt down before Master Zhang to express their deepest thanks, and she quickly had them stand back up. The entire audience was on their feet now and, as the thunderous applause continued, some tried to get a glimpse of the BB in the cup.

Boy with Myasthenia Gravis

Another fascinating case started out as a private session. Though it was not in front of an audience, the case ended up being publicized nevertheless. A fifteen-year-old boy who lived in Chaoyang City suffered from myasthenia gravis, a rare autoimmune neuromuscular disease. The boy's muscles lacked white ligaments, and he could not stand or walk. Of course, his parents had taken him to many hospitals and specialists over the years, but to no avail. Finally, they brought him to see Master Zhang.

When Master Zhang first saw the boy, she felt great sympathy for him but honestly admitted her concerns to his parents. "Let me try," she said, "but I am not sure that I can cure him." She then went through her process of manifesting medicine out of the air for the boy. It was an herbal powder. After taking the powder, the boy

International Recognition

tried his best to stretch his arms up, but couldn't. His parents knelt down before Master Zhang and encouraged her by saying, "Please do not hurry. The boy has been immobile for so many years that it is impossible to cure him in an instant. Please try again!"

Master Zhang was moved but also felt uneasy. She replied, "Okay, let me try again. After three days, carry the boy here once more and I will make up medicine for him a second time. After that, if there is no significant change, then you should not come to me again."

After three days, the parents brought the boy back, and the pressure to succeed could not have been greater because the Liaoning television station had sent a film crew to record the event. When Master Zhang saw the boy, she could tell there had been a slight improvement. She thought, *Maybe the medicine I produced was a little weak. This time, I should make up some liquid medicine for him. The liquid medicine is stronger and more effective.* So, she started her psychic powers and, after some effort, manifested liquid medicine from the air. Miraculously, after drinking the liquid medicine, the boy could move by himself!

This astonishing event was aired on both local and international television news stations and caused such a stir that Master Zhang was inundated with letters from the public.

Soon afterward, the boy started to walk slowly and gingerly and his parents visited Master Zhang to thank her again. Their son continued to improve and, at the age of twenty, was able to graduate from middle school. He could not walk smoothly like most people, but he was able to walk and take care of himself nevertheless—something he could never do before. No longer completely paralyzed, he had bright prospects for the rest of his life.

At one point, Master Zhang said, "I believed that the boy could recover from his illness because I knew that the cells helping the growth of his ligaments had grown up."

Blind Boy Says, "It's a Tiger!"

Mr. Yang, president of the Yangzi Company in Hong Kong, had something wrong with his heart. He had visited various hospitals for treatment but nothing had proven effective. In April of 1993, president Yang made a special trip from Hong Kong to see Master Zhang and ask for her help. She was able to quickly eliminate his illness and, with deep gratitude, he gave her a valuable gold watch as a gift. He also invested a billion yuan in Shenyang City, in Master Zhang's home province of Liaoning, to build a 5-star hotel and renovate the Changjiang Street. As part of his appreciation, he also invested in her hometown of Kezu for the construction of scenic spots.

One day, President Yang introduced a friend of his named Xue to Master Zhang. He said there was a boy in Xue's family who had become blind at the age of seven for no apparent reason. As usual, the family had visited many hospitals to no avail. Master Zhang agreed to see the boy, and when his family heard about her psychic powers, they were convinced it was the Buddha sending the wonderful Liaoning woman to cure the boy. The whole family awaited her arrival.

This time, upon president Yang's invitation, Master Zhang traveled to Hong Kong and Mr. Yang's house. Early in the morning, Xue's family brought the blind boy over. He was a sweet child and Master Zhang felt very sympathetic toward him. She went through her process of diagnosing, and the young boy asked her with hope, "Will my eyes be able to see again?"

Without hesitation, Master Zhang answered, "Yes!" As the boy welled up with tears of joy, he closed his eyes.

Master Zhang sensed there was something blocking the boy's optic nerve. So she waved her hand to get rid of the obstacle, patted his head, and declared, "Open your eyes! Look!"

The boy's parents were admittedly surprised at this quick declaration and thought, *Can blindness be cured in such a simple way?* Even Mr. Yang was surprised and skeptical. But, the little boy tentatively blinked his eyes and said, "I can see!" He immediately pointed to a picture and announced, "It's a tiger!" Then, when he turned around to see his parents, he said, "Why are you crying?"

Everyone in the room repeatedly praised Master Zhang, saying things like: "I cannot believe it!" "It's simply the living Buddha!" "The Buddhist Goddess comes to earth!" "It is a case of illness disappearing at the touch of a hand!"

Master Zhang attracted many more people who wanted healings during that stay in Hong Kong and she worked with as many as she could, and then with more in Taiwan before going back to China.

Nun Photographed in White Light

Through the end of 1993 and the whole next year, Master Zhang continued to give amazing performances and lectures to large audiences. In March of 1994, she was in Japan and decided to visit Hong Kong again on her way back to China. The Qing Ming Festival was occurring in Hong Kong and, at the same time, a meeting of the

Qing Ming Buddhist Congregation was being held and hosted by Master Yong Xing.

Master Yong Xing was the most popular Grand Master in the Hong Kong Buddhist community, and people used to call him "Senior Xing." He was more than seventy years old, and his hometown was Kezu County in the Liaoning Province of China, where Master Zhang lived. Master Xing was held in very high regard in Buddhist circles around the world for his teachings of the sutras.

As a Buddhist herself, Master Zhang felt very fortunate to have the opportunity to join this grand gathering in Hong Kong, and Master Yong Xing introduced her to many great Buddhist masters from Malaysia, Thailand, Singapore, and mainland China. They all enthusiastically greeted her with the heshi gesture.

The gathering was held on the fourth floor of the Pudi Association building and among the attendees was an old Buddhist nun in her eighties. She was thin and sat in pain on the floor as she stared at Master Zhang with bright, penetrating eyes. Tragically, the old nun had broken her left ankle three days before, and it was a complex fracture, with the bone broken in several places. This type of injury is very difficult to recover from, especially in the later stages of life, and can often disable a person.

Seeing this, Master Zhang sympathized with the old nun and made up her mind to help her if she could. Though there were many masters attending with high Buddhist powers, she was confident and determined to do her best. So, she washed her hands, lit some incense, put her palms together in the heshi gesture of respect, and prayed before a Buddhist sculpture with her pledge to cure the fracture. She mobilized her psychic powers to the utmost and started to sort out the broken bones and then set them, letting her own

International Recognition

qi energy penetrate into the relevant *xue wei* (acupuncture points, pronounced "shway-way").

A camera was recording the event. One minute, two minutes, ten minutes, finally a half hour went by before Master Zhang finished working on the old woman. She then wiped the sweat from her forehead and said to the nun, "Please stand up." All the attendees of the meeting looked anxiously at her. The old woman herself felt nervous and hesitated. She was worried she might break her bones even more if she tried to stand. But Master Zhang waved her hand and once again said, "Please Master, try to stand up. Do not worry about it. I am sure you can do it." At that point, someone else also encouraged her, saying, "Just try it!" Another person attempted to support the nun, but Master Zhang stopped him, saying, "Please—let her do it by herself."

So, the old woman bravely stood up. The audience broke out in cheers and Master Zhang instructed her, "Please come to me."

At first, the nun was afraid to walk. But she started moving her feet slowly, one step at a time. The room burst into thunderous applause! Many Buddhist masters in the room put their palms together with continuous praises, saying things like, "It's a miracle!" and, "It is an incarnation of Buddha!"

Master Zhang was very happy and, with tears in her eyes, finally felt she could rest and sit down on the sofa. After the applause subsided, she said to the gathering, "When one is truly kind-hearted, they can deeply move Heaven and get the assistance of special quantities of energy to perform unexpected miracles."

Afterward, some photographs of the nun that had been taken as she was being treated showed her almost completely obscured by white light. All that could be seen in the pictures were the flaps of her robes and her feet. Master Zhang says the white light was her own psychic energy and refers to an article written by Yang Yulin that appeared in the publication *Qigong and Health* on April 15, 1994. The article refers to scientific studies done on the transmittance of energy. It reported:

> Usually, the human body's radiation of visible light is very weak, but those who practice qigong can transmit strong light, even in different colors such as red, blue, purple, gray and gold. The light can be photographed by color film, and the person in possession of psychic powers can see this light. But its brightness cannot be compared to sunshine, so not everyone can see it. According to the aforesaid concept, we have cooperated with the Consultative Service Department of China Qigong Science Research Institute to use x-ray film and spectrometers to examine the energy transmitted by about a hundred qigong masters. The results proved that the qigong masters could transmit not only visible light, but also invisible light, such as infrared, ultraviolet, and x-ray.

Master Zhang stayed in Hong Kong for another five days after this meeting and provided healing treatments to about fifty people. She also held four press meetings to an audience of approximately 100,000 people.

Postman Vomits Up Cancer

In May of 1994, the Henan Qigong Science Research Institute invited Master Zhang to give a five-day presentation on psychic powers in the auditorium of the Post and Telegram Bureau. The auditorium was not large and could only hold about 500 people,

International Recognition

yet more than 1,000 came. Many temporary seats had to be placed along the corridors, causing a lot of hustling and bustling. Over the five days, Master Zhang taught the theory of psychic powers and the method of moving chi energy.

One of the attendees was a postman named Yun Jingxin, a native of Kaifeng City. He was in his prime, only about forty years old, but he had been diagnosed with terminal cancer of the esophagus. Yun Jingxin was desperate and had been looking everywhere for the possibility of a cure. So when he heard about Master Zhang's lectures on the Chinese Divine Powers, he felt a glimmer of hope. He bought a ticket and went to the meeting. Yun Jingxin described his experience afterward in the following way:

> After listening to the lecture on the first day, I did not feel any obvious changes except that my mood had become better. I saw the master making up medicine from the air, and it was 100 percent real. I thought to myself, *China has such a wonderful person in her. There should be no illness that cannot be cured.*
>
> On the second day, I felt very confident attending the meeting and was wishing I could get a Lucky Card. Unfortunately, the day passed, and I got nothing. I felt better during the day, but at night my chest felt more restricted and I could not eat anything. I thought, *Maybe I should not go tomorrow.* But more restriction might be a type of change that was good. So, even though I thought it might be in vain, I decided to go to the lecture again. I had already been sentenced to death, so what did I have to lose?
>
> After listening to the lecture on the third day and receiving the energy transmitted by Master Zhang, I felt good again. But by nighttime, my pain had increased.

Upon arising on the fourth day, I noticed the pain had decreased and it seemed that my illness had finally taken a turn for the better. So, I began to feel hope, ate breakfast, and went back to the meeting. While listening to the lecture that morning, I felt nauseous, like I was going to vomit. At the noon break, I saw many people around Master Zhang and she looked tired. Though I wanted to ask her for an individual treatment, I could not do it because of the crowd around her. Finally I gave up and the fourth day passed.

On the fifth and last day, I felt very good. Master Zhang was transmitting energy from the stage, and I sat under the stage and intentionally accepted her energy. When her energy was transmitted, I thought, *The cancer in my esophagus seems to be softening and decreasing.* I was thinking about this when suddenly my chest became very restricted, as if I were suffocating, and I felt a spasm of pain like a knife cutting through me. I thought, *I should not lose face in front of the audience and interrupt the meeting.* But I could not stop myself and began to vomit. *OOOAAHHHH.* Two small balls of flesh covered with saliva and something attached came out of my mouth! After that, my chest felt hot but not restricted.

The entire audience swarmed around me and the lecture workers came to me and picked up the things I'd vomited out. The audience squeezed in to have a look, and someone said repeatedly, 'It's a miracle! It's a miracle!' An examination later showed that what I had vomited were two cancerous tumors. I was very astonished and shouted, 'I am saved! I am saved!'

At that time, Master Zhang came to me and said, 'When you go back home, just eat some soft food, gruel, and milk powder. Rest for a few days; then you should be okay.'

Ten days passed very quickly. When Master Zhang came back from Puyang via Kaifeng, the public was enthusiastically asking for another presentation like that five-day lecture. She had to hold another meeting to fulfill the demands of the public. When I heard she would be here again, my wife and I went to visit her to let her know how I was doing. I told her, 'I am alright now and can eat food and take rest.' We wanted to express our gratitude to Master Zhang and tried to give her the money we had set aside for my funeral. She steadfastly refused it and replied, 'You have already spent a lot of money on your illness. How can I accept it? Please just get more rest, and then you can go back to work.'

My wife and I will never forget Master Zhang's kindness as long as we live. And I will practice the skill with the methods she taught me for the rest of my life.

Yun Jingxin's experience shows that not everyone needs to have an individual healing session to get well. Attending Master Zhang's workshops and practicing what she teaches can also be a way to achieve recovery. Receiving the energy she shares with the audience is healing in itself, but learning how to practice the Chinese Divine Powers and move chi on one's own can ensure good health for even longer.

CHAPTER 13

Communicating with Spirits

*I*NTERACTING WITH SPIRITS is part of everyday life for Master Zhang. Ever since she can remember, she has always seen spirits. As a young child, she often noticed them, especially during events such as funerals. But it wasn't until she was about twenty years old that she started talking to them. While doing her healing work, she regularly sees spirits—either around or attached to people. Those around people are usually guides of some sort who are helping the person. Those that are "attached" are spirits who have attached themselves to the person for their own reasons. They are not necessarily malevolent entities, but they could be causing the person harm nevertheless by interfering with his or her energy flow, health, or behavior. Master Zhang can either remove the attached spirit or spirits herself, or instruct the person as to how to perform a ceremony at home to make them leave and move on. And sometimes Master Zhang will tell people interesting information about the spirit guides around them.

THE DIVINE AND MASTER ZHANG

Talking to the Raven

But there is another type of spirit communication Master Zhang can do that is particularly intriguing. It is where Master Zhang speaks to a spirit in the language of spirits. It is not Chinese or any other language she was ever taught. This language simply came to her, appearing all at once in 1984. It was the day before the tornado hit, and she was feeling sad about how things were going with her new family. Unexpectedly, a spirit showed up and told her in this different language that a disaster would happen the next day. Master Zhang automatically understood the spirit language and from that time forward was able to speak it whenever she needed to. She says that when she speaks in this unusual tongue, she also sees a picture of everything being communicated, and this allows her to understand things even more clearly.

One time, when Master Zhang was with a small group of people, casually talking in someone's living room, this spirit language played a very important role. A large black raven flew up to a window of the house they were in. It tapped on the window, while looking in at the people. Everyone in the living room saw a big black raven . . . everyone, that is, except Master Zhang. What Master Zhang saw when she looked at the bird was the spirit of a young man wanting to get a message to one of his parents who was deeply grieving his death. So Master Zhang started talking to the raven (young man) in the special spirit language. Through her, he was able to get the message across to let his parents know he was fine and not to worry anymore.

When asked later, Master Zhang admitted she did not know if the young man's spirit spoke through a bird that had always been a bird, which then continued its life in physical form as a bird after the session, or if the young man's spirit temporarily showed itself in the form of the raven and then disappeared as a bird and returned to the spirit realm after the session. Master Zhang's guess was that the young man's spirit had temporarily transformed into this raven. This type of phenomenon is reminiscent of Native American lore and other shamanistic thinking around the world that sees nature and animals closely intertwined with the spiritual realms.

The Wandering Emperor's Spirit

One day in mid-June of 2002, Master Zhang was feeling tired after a long day of household chores that her mother-in-law had required of her, and she had just stopped for a short rest. Immediately, she fell into a trance. It looked like she had fallen asleep, but she hadn't. Even though Master Zhang was not fully asleep, however, she experienced a sort of dream vision. She clearly saw an older man with a kind countenance and mustache, who looked to be about seventy years old and from an ancient time.

The old man had come to communicate something important. He said he was Emperor Qian Long of the Qing Dynasty. (Emperor Qian Long was a real emperor of China who lived from 1711 to 1799.) He explained that his spirit had been left stranded abroad for many years and he now led a wandering life in the United States of America. Currently, he was staying in a household in Florida. The emperor relayed to Master Zhang the city, street address, and phone number of the household his spirit was stranded in. He wanted her to save him. He also said he had been waiting for many years, and that during this time he had found some other candidates who he thought might be able to help him, but they were either lacking in ability or destiny to do so. Thus, he had not been able to find anyone who was qualified. However, he told her that after investigating some more, he knew Master Zhang was the one most suitable.

Apparently, there was some unfinished business that was keeping the spirit of Emperor Qian Long at the Florida household and he wanted to entrust Master Zhang with the mission of finalizing that business. She wanted to know more details at this point, but her mother-in-law came in and aroused her from her trance state.

Master Zhang pondered the dream-like vision over and over. She had visited the United States several times by then, but knew nothing about the residential area the emperor had described or the business he wanted her to clear up. She had some doubts and wasn't sure what to do. However, whenever she remembered the semi-awake dream, she felt the old man was very sincere and that the information about the address and phone number of the household were clear. So, she could make a long-distance phone call to verify some things and after that make her decision. By making the phone call, she found out the old emperor's story appeared to be true.

Later that month, Master Zhang flew to Florida. After arriving, she found the house the emperor had indicated and spoke to a woman named Judy, who was the hostess of the home. Judy was related to an American army officer, now deceased, who had gone to Beijing in the Eight-Power Allied Forces in 1900. These were aggressive troops sent into China by Britain, the United States, Germany, France, tsarist Russia, Japan, Italy, and Austria. One of the tragedies was that during this invasion, the "Yuanming Yuan," or the Imperial Garden of Perfect Brightness, was burned down by the aggressors and its treasures looted. Judy's deceased relative, the American officer, was one of those who had stolen treasures from Yuanming Yuan and had brought them back to the United States.

Judy owned a pair of statues that were from this garden in Beijing. They were ivory sculptures, each more than a meter in height, on pedestals and carved with the images of Emperor Qian Long and his concubine. They were also engraved with Chinese characters that said, "Qian Long of Qing Dynasty" and "Lady of Qian Long." The sculptures were beautifully and meticulously carved and along with them was a porcelain vase in pea green and purple. Master Zhang bought the ivory sculptures and the porcelain vase from Judy and returned them to China. At the same time, she reported the event to the Chinese Consulate in America. She then felt the mission entrusted to her by Emperor Qian Long, who had died in 1799, was finally completed and his spirit was no longer stranded and looking for help.

A Visit From Kuan Yin

Master Zhang has had countless interactions with the high-level spirit being Kuan Yin, who is revered in China as the Bodhisattva of Mercy and Compassion. Kuan Yin came to Master Zhang virtually every night when she lived in a cave from age sixteen to eighteen and taught her the Buddhist sutras. But she continued to visit Master Zhang many times, and there was an interesting incident where Kuan Yin actually showed her presence to a large group of people.

It was at a park in China when Master Zhang was leading a group of students through a morning qigong movement. One of the students remarked that they had heard Kuan Yin would show herself if asked to do so. Another student asked Master Zhang if she would ask. So Master Zhang said she would, and there in the park she prayed for Kuan Yin to show herself. All the students looked up to the sky to see if a vision of some kind might appear. Master Zhang looked up, too. But when she lowered her eyes, she saw a flash of light on a nearby tree. "The Pusa (Kuan Yin) is revealing herself there," she said, and all the students went to look.

On the bark of this tree, small caterpillars or worms of some type had created the image of a woman! When everyone looked closely, they could make out what looked like a veil covering the head of a sitting female, hanging beads on the torso, a medicine bowl being held, and even legs and feet curled up beneath robes. Many of the students had cameras and lots of pictures were taken. It was a good thing, too, that photos were taken, because later that day, a park caretaker who had seen what happened burned the image from the tree trunk with a torch. Most likely this was a standard sort of response during the height of communism, when spirituality was aggressively suppressed.

Two Encounters With Jesus Christ

Many westerners may be interested to know that Master Zhang has experienced at least two encounters with Jesus Christ. (And hearsay suggests more than two.) The first encounter was in a dream, and the second was while she was awake.

As for the first encounter, her dream was about a beautiful church in Taiwan with a huge cross that she'd had the pleasure of visiting during one of her trips. In her dream, there was a big pool of water inside the church. It was beautiful and the water was bright blue. Jesus was standing there with a watering can like he was filling the pool with water from the can. She felt he wanted her to come to him and wash for a cleaner future. She understood that he was asking her to bathe in the water and be baptized. But in the dream, she was embarrassed to take off her clothes right in the middle of the church where someone might see her, and asked if she could do it in a smaller room instead. What if someone walked into the church and saw her naked? But Jesus answered, "No. You must do it here."

This is strange, she thought. *I'm not of the Christian faith. Why is he asking me to bathe in these waters and be baptized?* Finally, she gave in and started toward the pool of water. But rather than having her enter the water, Jesus walked over to her and poured blue water from his watering can over her head. Then she woke up.

After waking, Master Zhang wasn't sure if it had been just a dream or if it had really been a visit from Jesus Christ. She was convinced soon, however, that it was more than a dream when, at eight o'clock that morning, a group of seven or eight Christians showed up at her door. This was *not* a pre-arranged visit and she was surprised to see them, having no idea why they were there. They gave her a gift of a very special cross and red copper-type plaque with an image of a church, the Cross, and Jesus Christ on it. Then, the group of Christians prayed for Master Zhang and sang hymns to her. When they were done, they left just as mysteriously as they had arrived. This convinced Master Zhang it really *had* been Jesus in her dream, and she felt honored by his visit.

The next encounter she had, however, was *not* in a dream. She was fully awake and sitting in a church in a Chinese community of California, where the sermon was being given in Chinese. As Master Zhang was listening to the sermon, she saw the spirit of Jesus come down off the cross and stand right next to the pastor (or priest). Jesus looked directly at Master Zhang and started speaking to her. No one else could see or hear him, as far as she knew, other than herself.

To Master Zhang's recollection, Jesus said something like, "I went through all of that with the Cross, and look at what people do. The purpose was for peace and love. Yet, see how divided they all are . . . everyone separating into different religions and fighting each other!" He seemed unhappy with how people were treating each other. Master Zhang, of course, had not been raised in the Christian religion, but she nevertheless revered Jesus and sincerely asked him, "Are you like the Buddha?" Jesus answered something like, "In a way." He then said, "Buddhists build temples to pray in, and Christians build churches. It is all the same." And that was the end of her second encounter with Jesus Christ.

What Jesus said to her that day in the church supports how Master Zhang sees things as well. When asked about the large variety of religions on this planet, her answer is that there is a Chinese saying which claims,

> 10,000 different beliefs all come together eventually as one.

She believes that, no matter what a person's religious denomination, all spiritual traditions at their core are meant to teach each of us to be a kinder and better person. Thus, Master Zhang has no bias toward or against any particular religion. In fact, while being interviewed for this writing, she said at one point,

> The purpose of this book is not to become famous, but to leave a record for future scientists . . . and also to let people know that God and Jesus Christ exist. People think he died on the cross, but his soul lives on.

CHAPTER 14

Pearls, Turtles, and Teleportations

As Master Zhang became more and more well known, a broader extent of her abilities began to show, especially around her ability to teleport items from one place to another. This was particularly apparent in small group settings for educational purposes, or sometimes simply when she was having a good time with friends. Here are some fascinating examples.

Pearls for Everyone

In the latter part of March 1994, Master Zhang had been visiting Japan, and the head of a Japanese company, Mr. Zhang Yongxiang, offered to give her a sightseeing tour before she left. Zhang Yongxian (pronounced "Zhong Yong-SHAN") was a friendly, hospitable man who greatly appreciated her psychic powers. Master Zhang accepted his offer and proceeded on the tour along with Yongxian, his wife, and some of his staff.

It was a wonderful day to be out and Master Zhang was feeling very happy. They walked and walked, and Master Zhang was smiling the whole time. Suddenly, she stopped and turned around to her group of friendly hosts. With goodwill in her heart, she said, "Good friends, I would like to leave something for you as tokens of remembrance. Okay?"

Unanimously, they said, "That would be wonderful!" Then they admitted they'd been hoping for something like that but were too embarrassed to ask. The small group all stood around Master Zhang and looked at her expectantly. Stretching her hand out in front of her, she lightly caught something from the air. With her fist still closed she said, "What is this? Let's see." As she opened her hand, they saw in amazement that she was holding a handful of pearls! No one, of course, knew where the pearls had come from.

Master Zhang then told them, "Each of you can have a pearl." They all stretched out their hands, one after the other, and marveled at the pearls they had so graciously received. But there was still one pearl left in her hand. After checking, they were sure that each person had received a pearl, so why was there an extra one?

"Did you send someone out to buy melons for us?" Master Zhang asked.

"Yes, yes. One person is buying melons right now."

"The extra one belongs to him," she waved her hand and said.

The man who had gone out to buy melons was Mr. Shi, and he came hurriedly back with the melons in his arms. As he walked toward the group, he appeared agitated and shouted, "When I

Pearls, Turtles, and Teleportations

bought the melon, I found a pearl in my wallet! How did a pearl get in my wallet?"

No one made a sound, but everyone in the group quietly stepped closer to Master Zhang and looked at her hand. It was now empty. She had teleported the last single pearl to the man buying melons!

The whole group was in awe. But they were even *more* astonished when Master Zhang then instructed them, "Please examine your pearls and look carefully to see the inside of the pearl." After careful inspection, they exclaimed, "Ah! A Buddha statue. The Goddess of Mercy!"

Master Zhang then explained, "This is the Pearl Buddha. The Buddhist body is omnipresent in the universe and familiar with everything and everyone. Buddhist power has no bounds. All living creatures became obsessed with finding the truth through hearing and seeing, and since then the essence has been hidden. Only by good deeds, by being just and honest, can everybody be a Buddha. Please take your Pearl Buddhas!"

They all thanked her profusely and put their souvenirs carefully into their pockets next to their hearts. Everyone in the group admired her and thought she was a goddess and the living Buddha. Later, Mr. Zhang Yongxiang and his wife promised to build a Buddha statue in Master Zhang's hometown to let the Buddha light illuminate every corner of the land and to inspire "the ten thousand things of creation."

Three Turtles Appear

Earlier that month during the same trip to Japan, Master Zhang had performed what might be considered an even more impressive demonstration. She'd been invited to a gathering in a high-rise building, where she had successfully demonstrated her psychic powers. For example, she used her x-ray vision with a famous man named Kunchi Kanor and gave him the diagnosis: "You have a weak spleen and stomach, cold kidney, and *tinea manuum* on your feet" (a fungal infection caused by ringworms). He bowed to her and responded, "You are right! Thank you, Master Zhang."

Master Zhang couldn't help thinking, *Since I came to Japan, I have been warmly treated by my Japanese friends from many circles, and my psychic powers have been very successfully performed. In today's gathering, what can I do to repay their enthusiasm?*

Suddenly, she thought of a type of green sea turtle that used to be an auspicious (good) omen in Japan. Once she had that idea, she rubbed her hands together, recited some prayers, and, with her right hand waving in the air, she shouted, "Attention, please!"

All eyes were focused on her to see what she was going to do. As they were all wondering, she pulled some things out of the air and put them on the floor. Eyes bulged as the congregation looked down and saw three live sea turtles! One was the size of a plate, another the size of a bowl, and the last the size of a cup. So it looked like there were three generations of turtles freely crawling around on the floor!

One person said, "How could those turtles 'fly' to this twenty-third floor?" All the guests rocked with laughter, and someone shouted, "They are mascots of Japan and they have come for the celebration!" Loud cheers burst out. At the same time, the guests saluted Master Zhang with applause.

After the demonstration, everyone at the gathering went out to the ocean and set the turtles free. The three turtles started swimming out to sea but raised their heads up and looked at the people for a moment before they dove under the water. Master Zhang admits she does not know whether they were actually real turtles before she grabbed them out of the air or spirits of turtles that wanted to help her with her demonstration. Thus, they either continued their lives as turtles in the ocean, or they went back into spirit form after diving under the water.

Ancient Buried Coins

In November of 1996, Master Zhang went with some friends to visit a famous archaeological site in China called "Chaoyang Cave." Chaoyang Cave is actually made up of seventy individual caves running through Longfeng Mountain near Master Zhang's hometown. A beautiful place, there are tall cypress trees that appear to flourish with their roots in the stones. One impressive, large cypress is about 800 years old and is called "The first ancient cypress in northeast China." The caves are deep, with a year-round fresh spring, and all their entrances face East.

About 5,000 years ago, these caves were the residence of a people who lived between the Hong Shan and Xiajiadian cultures. These people of remote antiquity were highly psychic, and many were psychic from birth. Later on, with the development of society and scientific progress, their psychic powers gradually degenerated and the number of psychic individuals decreased. Still, over the years, the caves were often used for meditation. One famous monk named An Xiu meditated there in 1885. He was called the "Snow Monk" because he could walk on snow barefoot and meditate naked on a stone in winter.

Master Zhang and her friends climbed the mountain and were at the entrance to a large cave called Jin Chan Cave. As they walked around, they saw two huge stones covered with moss, both of which were shaped like toads. One toad-shaped stone looked up to Heaven, and the other looked down to the earth. Master Zhang walked up to the stone facing the ground and stretched out her hands with palms up and both hands linked together by the little fingers. She said, "There are some things here under the ground."

Her companions gathered around as she slowly closed her hands together into the heshi style of greeting. After a bit, she waved her hands and there was a sound. Then she asked them, "Would anyone like to guess what is in my hands?" Finally, upon her instruction, one of her friends came over and pulled something out from between her fingers that was rusted and in the shape of a knife. Then another similar item was pulled out from between her hands, and another. One member of the group who was knowledgeable about historical things examined the three items and stated, "They are knife-shaped coins. In ancient times, there were knife-shaped coins, used most likely during the Warring States period." Master Zhang had psychically *known* something was under the ground at that particular point and then used her own powers to teleport the items up into her hands!

Later, the three coins were taken to Beijing for examination by archaeologists and were confirmed as authentic.

Getting Change

It was August 5, 1992 at about nine o'clock at night in Kezu County. Master Zhang was at the house of a man named Sun Guibao, treating him for osteomyelitis, which he'd had for more than two years. The bone infection was debilitating and he could not stand or walk. Some members from the I & R Team were also with her at Sun's house. Master Zhang started up her psychic powers and on her "mental screen" saw a dim black shadow appear behind Sun Guibao's image. So she knew the cause of the illness.

Master Zhang proceeded to ask Sun's family members for more information. "Did any of your ancestors serve in the army or carry out a robbery?"

"No" was the answer.

Then she said, "Do not be shy. Just state the facts."

"Oh," one said, "I remember now that one of our ancestors was a robber."

"Ah!" she replied. "Robbers and other criminals that do bad deeds should be punished by law and the acts never permitted by Heaven. That the father's debt should be paid by his son is perfectly justified."

"What can we do then? Please find a way for us."

Master Zhang thought for a while and said, "Okay, let's do this. The patient is seriously ill and it is difficult to cure him right now. I think we should first perform an emergency treatment by letting him have an *an gong* pill (a particular type of herbal medicine common in China). But in order to avoid any low-quality an gong pills, we had better get it from the well-respected Tong Ren Dang pharmacy. Let me try to move the medicine from there to here. If this can be done, then there is hope for him. If the medicine is not available, however, then his illness is incurable. Let us see what the heavens determine. The heavens' decision should not be disobeyed."

Master Zhang then restarted her extrasensory perception and, in less than three minutes, a pack of an gong pills dropped down on the window sill. Everyone in the house was stunned and Sun's family members dropped down on their knees in gratitude.

Master Zhang then shocked them even more by saying, "The medicine is here so we should pay for it now."

"How can we pay for it?" they asked. "The Tong Ren Dang Pharmacy is in Beijing, more than 10,000 li from here!" Also, it was after closing hours for most pharmacies.

"It's easy," Master Zhang explained. "You put the money on the window sill and I will send it back. The correct change will remain here."

So the family members placed one hundred yuan on the window sill and Master Zhang waved her hand. Everyone in the room stared as 78 yuan and change disappeared from the sill and twenty-one yuan and change remained!

Two Flasks of Water

On November 5, 1993, a provincial TV station correspondent came to visit Master Zhang. He was accompanied by others, including Chairman Wu of the County Federation of Literature and Art. They all met at a restaurant. Chairman Wu was in quite a good mood and wanted his friends to see a demonstration of Master Zhang's psychic powers. She complied and began by using her x-ray vision to diagnose a friend of his, a man named Old Li. Chairman Wu was excited and winked at his friends in the restaurant. Immediately, the staff and other customers at the restaurant came into the room to see what was happening. Soon, the place was full of observers. One of the restaurant staff was a man named Yu, who was skeptical.

Pearls, Turtles, and Teleportations

Master Zhang rolled up her sleeves and stretched out her five fingers on both hands in the air to show that her hands were completely empty. Then she closed her hands into the heshi Buddhist greeting. She opened her hands again and blew a puff of breath on her palms, murmured some prayers, and shouted, "Old Li, please take the medicine!"

Old Li stood up, bowed, and waited. With everyone looking on, she dropped a red pill into Old Li's hands. He held the medicine with surprise and let the audience look at it. The red pill was soft and emitted a very strong herbal smell. Everyone was surprised and the skeptical worker, Yu, kept shaking his head, mumbling over and over, "It's incredible, incredible!"

Enjoying her presentation and wanting to put on a good show for Chairman Wu and his friends, Master Zhang then announced, "Please take two thermos flasks and fill them with boiling water." The restaurant manager quickly carried in two thermos bottles of boiling hot water. Then she said, "Someone can taste it first. It is plain boiled water, right?"

As the audience looked on, someone tasted the water in each flask and replied, "Yes!" Master Zhang then wrote the numbers "1" and "2" on the flasks to differentiate them. Everyone was wondering what she was going to do next.

"Now I am going to change the water in flask number one into medicine water," she announced and waved her hands in the air. She never touched the flask.

"Come and smell the water in flask number one." Those watching took turns smelling the strong Chinese medicine aroma in flask number one and they verified that flask number two still had plain hot water in it, with no aroma. Master Zhang then spoke again and said, "Now I am going to move the medicine water in flask number one to flask number two, and the hot water from flask number two into flask number one." Again, she did not touch either flask of water. She then followed that statement with, "Now, please take a look. Do you all agree that the liquid medicine has now been moved to flask number two?"

The observers examined the two flasks and confirmed, "Yes. The plain boiled water is now in flask number one, and the liquid medicine is in flask number two!"

Then Master Zhang changed the plain boiled water into medicine water as well and exclaimed, "Now, let's drink it." Chairman Wu tasted a little and said, "What a strong herbal flavor!" In fact, the whole restaurant was permeated with the aroma of Chinese herbal medicine. Everyone else wanted to taste it and all were given a chance. Someone said, "She is a Buddhist goddess!" Another said, "It's really divine liquid medicine!"

Chairman Wu made a speech congratulating Master Zhang and it was quite an evening. Even the stubborn worker, Yu, filled a little bottle with the liquid medicine to take home to his wife. He quietly whispered to Master Zhang, "I am convinced!"

Money Materializes

Of course, demonstrations of Master Zhang's powers were always popular, but one such event was especially notable. It was in front of some high officials in China in 1996, and there was also a reporter on the scene observing the demonstration. The officials were very curious about what she could do and wanted to see if she could bring

Pearls, Turtles, and Teleportations

money in from another location. So, Master Zhang had someone spread clean newspapers on the floor in front of the group. Without any difficulty at all, she caused $70,000 (in U.S. dollars) to materialize onto the newspaper.

The cash was probably from the reserves of some bank, but the exact source of it was not clear. Master Zhang did not want to steal the money or cause any alarm over it being missing, so she quickly sent all the money back to wherever it came from.

A reporter on the scene later sent a letter to the authorities describing what had transpired. In his letter, he asserted emphatically, "We have to study this person!"

Chapter 15
Trouble in Taiwan

—m—

ONE DAY IN THE MID-1990S, Master Zhang was busy doing her healing work in China when she suddenly received a message from the universe asking her to perform her good deeds more widely. The way she experienced it was two lines of words appearing on her mental screen that read:

> Let your kindness and open heart affect not only those who ask for help before you, but also let more people in the world who are in need perceive your genuine love.

She had already been traveling and giving presentations throughout Asia, but it wasn't until 1998 that she decided to start visiting the United States. It was around this time the Chinese government began exerting a heavy hand on large organizations that could end up amassing too much political power by the sheer fact of having large numbers of members. The Communist Party was also targeting anything strongly spiritual. One such group that was not at all political, but had amassed millions of members, was a peaceful group practicing a type of qigong that had become extremely popular called *Falun Gong*. Falun Gong was a discipline that combined meditation with slow qigong movements and a moral philosophy that emphasized truthfulness, compassion, and forbearance. Literally thousands of types of qigong practice have been taught in China, but Falun Gong differed from others in its focus on morality and its absence of fees or formal membership. The discipline usually took place outdoors in parks or on university campuses, and millions of people enjoyed gathering in large groups throughout China on a daily basis to practice.

In 1999, the Chinese government initiated a heavy-handed attack on Falun Gong aimed at eliminating the practice entirely. Estimates have been made that hundreds of thousands of Falun Gong practitioners were arrested and cruelly detained in prisons or labor camps.

Since part of the attack on Falun Gong was allegedly due to its spiritual nature, other practitioners of spiritual work were also at risk. In fact, at one point, Master Zhang was on a trip outside of China when she received a phone call from an official in Beijing who told her, "Don't come back to China right now because your name is on a list and they'll arrest you." Luckily, four or five days later, the same official called her back and said, "Now you're okay." Apparently, the Communist Party had realized she was not a typical qigong practitioner and was not political in any way. They realized she was totally different from others on the list and not a threat to the government. So, Master Zhang was able to return home.

But she did manage a two-year visit to the United States, from the end of 1998 to the end of 2000. Master Zhang was invited by

Trouble in Taiwan

the American College of Theology and the American Imperial University of Medical Sciences to give lectures twice a week. Upon completion of these lectures, she received certificates awarding her a Doctor of Divinity degree from the American College of Theology, and a Doctor of Philosophy degree in Alternative Therapy from the American Imperial University of Medical Sciences.

Then, at the end of 2000, Master Zhang was invited by a Taiwanese woman she'd met in the United States to visit Taiwan with her. The woman, Ms. Xue Sitao, was delighted to host Master Zhang in her hometown of Taipei, Taiwan, and this gave Master Zhang an opportunity to visit her own husband's relatives as well. In Taipei, Master Zhang performed healing sessions for some of Ms. Xue's relatives and some of her own in-laws. These were all a great success, and one famous journalist named Li Zongyou of the *Taipei China Post* heard about the healings. He interviewed Master Zhang on January 1, 2001, and watched her materialize medicine from the air. Others were there with the journalist as well, totaling about twenty people. One of them was the Dean of Studies of a Taiwan University, named Li Yitong, who had formally studied psychic powers for many years. The journalist, the Dean, and everyone else present were all astonished at what Master Zhang could do.

The University Dean, who had already written articles about psychic phenomena and even authored a book in which he quoted the classics and authoritative works about psychic abilities, could only say, "I do not know how to interpret what is happening. What I would like to say is that it is the Buddha sending the medicine." A young Taiwanese girl, Gao Qiaowu, who was also there and had psychic abilities herself, added, "I only saw a white light shining down, and the medicine was dropped down from her hands."

The next day, Li Zongyou's article appeared on the first page of the *China Post* in Taiwan. The title was *A Hand of Genius Taking Medicine from the Air*, and the date it came out was January 2, 2001. In it, Li Zongyou described his interview with Master Zhang and her performance of psychic powers.

That article shook all of Taiwan!

Media Craze and TV Show

Ms. Xue Sitao had a relative in the press who'd seen her performance and asked if she could do a healing session on a man with cirrhosis of the liver. The man was in critical condition and Master Zhang agreed to see him. She first asked him, "Do you want to live?" He answered painfully, "Yes!" Then she said, "If you want to live, the illness can be cured." So, she manifested some powdered medicine from the air to be taken every day for nine days and explained to the man, "You should be cured on the ninth day." By the eighth day, his illness was cured and he left the hospital to go home.

This story about the man with cirrhosis of the liver now spread rapidly through all the press circles of Taiwan, and the anchorwoman of a television station, Ms. Li Yanqiu, invited Master Zhang to be on her show. Thus, that night, Master Zhang appeared on Dong Shen TV and successfully demonstrated her ability to materialize medicine from the air. The TV show caused another big stir and a constant stream of newspaper journalists sought out Master Zhang for interviews and repeat performances.

But all of this went against Master Zhang's plans of spending only one week in Taiwan to pay a short visit to her husband's family, do a little sightseeing, and repay Ms. Xue's boundless hospitality.

It would be inconvenient for her to accept all the new invitations coming at her that would prolong her stay. Therefore, she rejected them and prepared to return to the United States.

As soon as people heard that Master Zhang was going to leave Taiwan, however, many were anxious to get healing sessions before she left. So Ms. Xue took it upon herself to organize appointments with advanced deposits for those who were eager to have healing sessions, and many, many advance appointments were set up. At the same time, Ms. Xue's brother-in-law, a military general, along with a Taiwanese celebrity, invited Master Zhang to perform her psychic powers in a setting arranged by the media.

When Master Zhang arrived at the venue, she immediately noticed many cars parked outside and the inside packed with more than seventy representatives from the media waiting for her. She also noticed two people wearing sunglasses on the stage. She was told the two men were magicians who were there to authenticate whether her performance was real or a sham.

When Master Zhang sat in the chair placed for her on the stage, she discovered it was on wheels and kept sliding backward. Before she even had time to complain about the chair, the two men in sunglasses came over to her, grabbed her hands, and accused her of having something hidden in her hands. They forcefully opened her hands while a few others jumped up onto the stage to assist the men. But all they discovered was that her hands were completely empty. Embarrassed, the men then started searching around the stage for the herbal medicine she was supposedly going to conjure up. Finally they had to stop their search and admit there was nothing there.

Master Zhang was understandably furious and berated the men saying, "I was invited by you to give a performance of psychic powers, and I always wash my hands before a performance. Without washing my hands, I cannot make up the medicine from the air. What you have done is rude and has humiliated me. You know nothing about psychic powers, and your foolish fancies have proven your ignorance."

Unfortunately, Master Zhang was so upset that it seriously affected her mentally and emotionally, and she was then *unable* to make up any medicine from the air. Of course, all the members of the media were very disappointed, and members in the audience who'd paid for advance appointments with Master Zhang complained heartily. Until then, Master Zhang had not known her friend, Ms. Xue, had organized the advance appointments by selling tickets and in such a way that would allow Ms. Xue to make a profit. When Master Zhang found out, she became very upset at this as well and left the venue angrily.

Unfair Detention

The two magicians and many journalists followed Master Zhang to where she was staying and made a scene because they had gotten nothing out of the event. Then, unfortunately, a television station broadcast the event as a scandal. Master Zhang tried to ignore all the media harassing her, but they were relentless and stayed outside her place day after day for a chance to interview her. Master Zhang's relatives advised her to get away somehow to avoid more trouble, and word got out she was going to leave Taiwan and go back to the United States. Someone in political authority with ulterior motives denied her departure from Taiwan, accusing her of *making up medication treatment without a license*. Master Zhang was officially arrested in Taiwan for that reason and for supposedly swindling people out of their money. Though she was not put in jail or imprisoned, she was detained and could not leave the country.

Someone then tried to frame Master Zhang by bribing people who'd had healing sessions with her to claim wrongdoing. But none of them would do it. They all took the stance that Master Zhang had given them the medicine free of charge and had healed their illnesses, and they would not do evil against their conscience. Not one of those treated in Taiwan would write a false statement about her.

Without complaints from the public, the government authorities had no way out. But they tried to trip her up by saying, "You are a psychic. Do you have a certificate?" To this, Master Zhang replied, "Not only do I not have a certificate for being a psychic, but the whole of society does not issue such a certificate! That I can see into bodies to cure illnesses is a fact, though I have no certificate." Then she added, "In Taiwan, I provided medication treatment to four people over two and a half days. You can ask them and get the proof."

The authorities had no reply to this, but they kept her under arrest anyway and continued to ask her the same questions over and over. "Do you have a license? Did you accept fees?" They continued to detain her in Taiwan and the situation became very serious. It dragged on and on to the point where the judge responsible for investigating Master Zhang was discharged because he had only a half-year post and a new judge had to be assigned.

Pills in the Court Room

Eventually, Master Zhang's case went to the Supreme Court of Taiwan. There were five judges and one prosecutor. One of them said, "You are psychic and can make medicine from the air. I do not believe it." Master Zhang said to him, "If I make it, will that make everything okay?" He said, "If I say 'okay,' then it will be okay." All the others agreed. So, right in front of the judges and prosecutor, Master Zhang produced two pills out of the air. The pills were sent for laboratory testing and Master Zhang had to wait a full two months for the results. On her final day in court, there were more than thirty journalists in the room to report the conclusion of her case. The laboratory testing of the pills revealed they were completely herbal and had no pharmaceutical components in them at all. The court concluded that her troubles had been caused by the media and one of the judges told her, "You were totally framed by the lawyers." Since she had been forced to undergo a year and a half imprisonment in that country, Master Zhang was awarded by the court a sum of three hundred thousand *taibi* in compensation and pronounced free to go.

Looking back at her long ordeal, Master Zhang says, "Just like that, I was wrongly sentenced in Taiwan and kept under arrest for a year and a half. It was the most humiliating experience of my life!"

Chapter 16
Coming to America

—m—

*I*N ACCORDANCE WITH HER earlier message from the universe to perform good deeds more widely, Master Zhang decided to spend more time in America. Her two-year visit to the United States before her trip to Taiwan had gone well and she now had connections in California. But would she risk accusations similar to those she had faced in Taiwan? Being accused of fraud and of practicing medicine without a license was a nightmarish ordeal and a dishonor she did not want to ever experience again. Fortunately, the Taiwan Supreme Court had pronounced her *not* guilty of those accusations. But a year and a half of her life had been stolen in the process. So Master Zhang made sure, while in the United States, to stay within the bounds of spiritual healing and energy work, and to never claim she can cure diseases.

Following are descriptions of some spiritual healing sessions that Americans have had with Master Zhang. Only the names have been changed to protect the individuals' identities.

The Spirit Wolf and Black-Haired Guide

Sarah, a young single woman, was twenty-five years old when she heard about Master Zhang and went to see her. She didn't have any serious physical problems but was in the process of building a broader outlook on life and decided to get a session with Master Zhang for spiritual input and possible healing. Sarah had done some shamanic work in Thailand the summer before where her two main spirit guides had been revealed to her. They were a large gray-and-white wolf and a beautiful, petite woman with long black hair that appeared to be of either Native American or Oriental descent. In Thailand, Sarah had also learned that the female spirit guide's name was Shelia (pronounced "SHEE-lia"). Just before sitting down with Master Zhang, Sarah used the restroom and quietly asked the gray wolf and Shelia to be present with her in the session.

Without knowing anything about Sarah's history, Master Zhang began to scan her body, starting from her head and moving down, as she usually does. Nothing serious or out of balance in her energy flow showed up, since Sarah was an active and healthy young woman. But Master Zhang did see that Sarah had broken her right ankle years before and that it had healed up fine. (Sarah later confirmed the broken right ankle was the only serious injury she'd ever had.)

Then, Master Zhang's eyes started moving away from Sarah and began looking around her. She said, "There is a dog" and asked Sarah if she had a gray-and-white dog. Sarah said she *did* have a dog, but it was almost completely black, not gray and white. Master Zhang responded, "No, it is gray" and insisted adamantly that Sarah must have had a gray-and-white dog at some point. Finally Sarah said, "Oh, are you talking about a dog in spirit?" Master Zhang said, "Yes," and that she could see it had just gone over and curled up on the floor in the corner of the room. Then, Sarah understood and replied, "That's my wolf spirit guide!" She explained to Master Zhang how she had done some shamanic work and gotten in touch with two of her spirit guides, one of which was a large gray-and-white wolf.

Then Sarah told Master Zhang about her black-haired female spirit guide named Shelia and Master Zhang confirmed, "Yes—she's here, too." Master Zhang was able to communicate with Shelia and reported, "She says you don't ask her for help enough." So Master Zhang explained to Sarah that whenever she needs guidance or help on anything, she should light two candles and ask Shelia for the help she needs. If the issue is serious, then Sarah should light three candles.

This information was intriguing to Sarah and she later began seeking help and guidance from her female spirit guide the way Master Zhang had explained. And it did help her in her life. With gratitude and appreciation, Sarah then had a picture of what she thought her black-haired spirit guide looked like tattooed on her arm! She also had a beautiful wolf image tattooed on her back.

One last thing that came out of this session was that, at the end of it, Sarah asked Master Zhang, "Am I going to get married?" Master Zhang laughed and said, "Yes, and you already know him." Sarah's first reaction was to feel disappointed. She thought, *Oh, no! I only know losers!* Apparently, her dating experiences to that point had not gone well. So Sarah was not happy with the answer Master Zhang gave her. However, two years later, Sarah started dating someone wonderful and this time it quickly became a very serious relationship, with talk of marriage. It wasn't until after Sarah started seeing the man that she suddenly realized he was, indeed, someone she had dated for a short time about five years before. Back then, they had liked each other very much but had conflicting lifestyles and weren't as compatible as they were now. She'd forgotten about this particular man during her session with Master Zhang!

Severe Edema

Lynda from California had a very unusual problem. She had developed an extreme case of edema (fluid retention) all over her body. By the time Lynda reluctantly saw Master Zhang for help, she was in a very bad state. She was only forty-three years old and had been perfectly healthy before this problem started. Her husband had taken her to all the medical specialists possible, yet none of them could figure out what was wrong with her. Lynda had gotten MRIs as well as every other medical test the doctors could think of, but the water retention just kept getting worse.

It had originally started in her feet, with each foot feeling like it weighed ten pounds. The edema had then spread throughout her entire body to the point where her legs were so stiff they wouldn't bend at the knees, and her arms were so stiff they would hardly bend at the elbows. Every place on her body was stretched to the limit and hard as a rock to touch. Because nothing would bend, Lynda couldn't pick her feet up off the ground and had to gingerly shuffle around, often tripping and crying. She couldn't feed herself because her elbows wouldn't bend, and it was a nightmare to try to sit down on a toilet because her knees wouldn't bend. To say that she was desperate would have been an understatement.

Lynda and her husband were beekeepers and had both been stung by bees several hundred times over the years, so most of the doctors thought that was probably what was causing this strange affliction. But the medical experts had no solutions. Consequently, Lynda had suffered miserably for more than a year, and not a single medical specialist could help her. Some doctors cruelly claimed her problem was "all in her head." One doctor merely said to her, "You're dying." Another, who was a cardiologist, said, "Your heart will not withstand this pressure much longer." Finally, she realized she probably had only about six months to live.

Lynda was, and still is, a very devout Christian, and seeing someone like Master Zhang for help was completely outside her belief system. But she had nowhere else to turn. So, when she heard about a group meditation an enigmatic healer from China was giving, she went. Lynda couldn't get close enough to Master Zhang to speak with her personally because she could only shuffle and everyone else was getting in front of her and blocking her way. However, she later found a way to see Master Zhang for a private session. Lynda's husband wasn't too happy about this decision because it was outside his comfort zone as well. So he stayed in the car while Lynda shuffled toward the house for her healing session.

Lynda admits that, at first, she was terrified. Master Zhang looked inside her body, psychically received information about her condition, and then, with wide-eyed Lynda watching, manifested herbs out of the air for her to take home. She did not see any specific disease and also did not promise she could cure her. She said only that, if the herbs helped, it would take time. When Lynda saw Master Zhang make the herbs materialize out of the air, it was all Lynda could do to keep from bolting out the door! The only thing that kept her there was looking into Master Zhang's eyes. Somehow, staying locked on those kind eyes gave Lynda the courage to stay put. Later, when Lynda looked back on the situation, she said, "I had to design a whole new level of faith because this was outside my belief system."

Master Zhang did tell Lynda in a general way, however, that it looked like her body was attacking itself and she might not be processing proteins correctly. She also said that when Lynda had had a car accident several years before, a mischievous spirit had attached itself to her, and the influence of that spirit had weakened her system. Master Zhang said it would take about a year for her body to heal itself. Lynda didn't know what to think and was still very scared. But it was the *only* time so far that anyone had given her even the slightest hope. So she went home and started taking the herbs from the Medicine Buddha.

Lynda took a small dose of the herbs in water at 9 p.m. every night for nine nights in a row. When anyone asks her what happened next, she replies, "Have you ever seen a horse pee?" Within about twenty minutes of taking the initial dose of herbs, she immediately had to shuffle to the bathroom as fast as she could. Straddling the toilet awkwardly, she claims the water flowed out of her like a fire hose! The next night, shortly after taking the herbs, the same thing happened. And it kept happening for nine days straight. By the end of the first week, Lynda could already feed herself and use the toilet normally. What a miracle!

Lynda had two more sessions with Master Zhang that year and by the one-year mark, was much, much better. At the two-year point, she was back to normal except for a slight heart murmur that had been caused by the physical stress of that much fluid retention for so long. Overall, Lynda lost fifty to sixty pounds of fluid during her recovery. She is incredibly grateful to be alive and encourages anyone needing help to keep their mind open to modalities that may be different from what they are used to.

A Headless Demon and Spider Spirit

In 2013, Celeste was very sick with multiple illnesses. In fact, she was near death at times. This unfortunate young woman was battling both Lupus and Lyme Disease. She was also trying to get back on her feet following a serious blood infection associated with a miscarriage.

Life was definitely *not* going well for Celeste. Her problems had become serious ten years earlier, when she'd been in a bad car accident. Injuries from that accident hit her particularly hard because she'd already been physically depleted from grieving the sudden, unexpected death of her father on Christmas Day. Moreover, her very strange uncle had cursed her the day before the accident. She didn't know why he did this, except that he was mentally unstable, and she wondered if the curse had actually caused her car accident.

Celeste had been to many doctors, but none of them could do much for her. As a last resort, one of her friends suggested she see Master Zhang. Celeste definitely did not want to go to this appointment. In telling her story, she explained, *I was super skeptical because I'd heard about fake healers who used sleight of hand to make their healing work seem more impressive. But I had run out of options, so I went. I was still unsure when I walked into Master Zhang's house. As soon as I entered the small room where she does sessions, however, I felt a powerful energy and was very affected when I looked into her eyes.*

Right away, as Celeste sat down, Master Zhang touched the back of her head and said, "You had a car accident and a concussion, and this is where it hurts." And she was right. Then, when Master Zhang scanned Celeste's body with her psychic sight, she saw inflammation in Celeste's brain, spirochetes (Lyme bacteria), evidence of Lupus, and toxins in every organ. Except for the organ toxicity, her doctors had already diagnosed everything else, and Celeste was amazed at Master Zhang's accuracy. Master Zhang also noticed that Celeste had the inherited gene for breast cancer with latent or dormant cancer cells stuck in her lymph system. Celeste already knew that some of the other women in her family had this gene and she'd been planning to get tested for it. Master Zhang also remarked that Celeste had had a miscarriage and suffered a bad infection. That was also true.

With every one of Celeste's physical ailments pointed out, Master Zhang then went into the spiritual aspects of her health problems. What came out shocked Celeste. Master Zhang said, "There is a headless demon around you" and remarked that she'd never seen this before. It was unclear as to why this spirit was there, but Master Zhang felt it was a very serious problem. She explained, "This will kill you. It will take you down. But don't worry—I can help you get rid of it." Master Zhang also saw three spirit entities around Celeste from family members and noted that one of Celeste's family members had used a negative entity to cause her to have the car accident. Celeste immediately thought of how her uncle had cursed her the day before the accident!

At the end of the session, Master Zhang showed Celeste how to do a special ceremony to rid herself of the unwanted spirits. She also manifested two different herbal powders out of the air for Celeste. One of the powders was brown in color and the other was white. Master Zhang said the white powder was to eliminate the dormant cancer cells stuck in her lymph system so they would not activate into breast cancer. Celeste noticed that Master Zhang was not wearing long sleeves and there was no way any sleight of hand could have been involved. At home, she performed the ceremony that had been indicated and experienced some intense grief, followed by relief and feeling much better.

A few weeks later, Celeste went to Master Zhang for a follow-up session. She had just come back from a trip to Chicago, where she'd been visiting relatives who all felt horrible because they were dealing with a family tragedy. For some reason, Celeste started to feel as though something was trying to crawl out of her skin. She saw another healer who intuitively saw a spikey, lobster-like spirit in her but didn't know what to do about it. When Celeste got home and had her follow-up session, Master Zhang saw the spirit immediately as well and remarked, "Yes, you have a spider spirit" and told Celeste it was feeding off her pain and fear. Master Zhang then showed her how to do yet another unique ceremony to get the spider spirit to go away. Luckily for Celeste, the ceremony worked.

It is possible that the reason multiple entities had been able to attach themselves to Celeste was because she had been so weakened by her numerous illnesses. She also learned that when Master Zhang first came to the United States, she was shocked by how many unreleased spirits there were in America. Apparently she could see many, many more entities around Americans than she had seen around people in China and other Asian countries. Master Zhang finally came to believe this is because Americans do not have a culture of "releasing." In Asian countries, there are ceremonies that people regularly perform to release entities from themselves and their homes. For instance, most Chinese families perform a ceremony every forty-nine days to release spirits. They also go to sites of death, such as where bad car accidents have occurred, and perform ceremonies to release the spirits that may be lingering there. This is truly a foreign concept to the modern western world, but it might be a good idea to look into.

Though Celeste was not completely cured of her Lyme Disease and Lupus, the spiritual healing work Master Zhang did with her clearly helped her body become stronger and her energy more balanced. For this reason, she continued to get sessions with Master Zhang until the symptoms of the Lupus and Lyme were so greatly reduced that she felt much better. She was then strong enough to undergo some other treatments that helped her return to a completely normal state of health.

A Vindictive Mother Spirit

Sam, a high-powered businessman and CEO, did not expect to have a life-changing experience when he attended a healing retreat in Mexico. In fact, he didn't even want to attend at all because it was Super Bowl weekend and he would miss the football game. Plus, he had no desire to travel to Mexico. But Sam had promised his wife he would accompany her to this exclusive event that was promoted for its interesting array of healers. The healers included a tai chi master, a monk, an acupuncturist, a shaman, and of course, Master Zhang.

At six-foot-three and 275 pounds, Sam had a formidable presence that was underscored by the no-nonsense air of the football player and cop he had been. He came from a rough childhood, in which he had been beaten regularly as a boy, mostly by his mother, who would even wake him up out of bed at times to give him a beating. And he was mistreated by his siblings as well. So, Sam was guarded. In his own words, Sam explained, "I've been full of anger all my life but learned how to control it—and I built a big, impenetrable shield around myself." Sam admitted he was also a "stress eater" and regularly turned to tequila to relax.

Since Sam had actually seen Master Zhang work before, her abilities did not surprise him. But during his first spiritual healing session with her at this retreat, he was nevertheless stunned by how accurate she was in her descriptions of some of the physical conditions his doctor had already diagnosed. For example, she said his blood was thick, and Sam's doctor had already reported that his hematocrit level was high.

But when Master Zhang started describing some spirits around Sam, the session took a dramatic turn. One of the spirits was his own mean mother, who had passed away twenty years before! Master Zhang said, "Your mother is on your back." Then, she started to communicate with Sam's mother in the language of the spirits that she knew so well. Master Zhang asked Sam's mother to leave him alone and move on. But she was very obstinate and would not leave.

Master Bruce Sun, the tai chi and qigong expert at the retreat and a renowned healer in his own right, was the only other person there who spoke both Chinese and English, so he acted as interpreter for Master Zhang. Thus, a strange interplay of languages began. Master Zhang would first speak to Sam's mother in the special language of the spirits she had learned years earlier. Then, she would have to tell Master Bruce in Chinese what she said and how Sam's mother responded. Then, Master Bruce would finally relay the whole interaction to Sam in English.

Through this unusual interplay of three languages, it was revealed that Sam's mother was in limbo as a spirit and was also *very* angry about a lot of things. One of the things she was angry about was that she had been buried in an old dress and not a new one. This was not surprising since she'd always been angry about everything all her life and had always been quite stubborn, according to Sam. Master Zhang continued to talk to the mother to find out more about her and why she would not leave.

Master Zhang said, "She loves vodka," which Sam verified. Then Master Zhang said she smelled smoke, and Sam said, "Yeah, my mother smoked." Master Zhang went on. "She loves money, and she loves to garden with those little packets of seeds." Sam said all of that was true, and Master Zhang remarked, "We need to get her off your back! There is a very, very angry little boy in you."

At this point, Master Zhang went back to speaking directly to the mother. She kept saying, "Let him go!" But his mother's spirit refused to leave him. So Master Zhang was forced to try to negotiate. She asked, "What do you want?" Sam's mother said, "I want a new dress, I want a drink, and I want my cigarettes." Then, she added, "And I want money." At first, she requested fifteen thousand dollars. Then she immediately upgraded the request to seventy-five thousand and then to one hundred fifty thousand dollars! Sam said that sounded like her. Quickly, she added that she also wanted cake and candy (she always kept candy nearby), alcohol, cigarettes, and seeds for planting. Sam admitted that all of this perfectly described his mother because she'd been a chain smoker, loved vodka, was always trying to get more money out of people, and yet, ironically, also loved working in her garden with little packs of seeds! Thus, he knew his mother was truly there.

However, the intensity of the session *really* peaked when Master Zhang relayed to Sam, "Your mother is trying to kill you. She's making you stress eat and drink too much because she wants you to join her!" At this point, the emotional intensity was so high that Sam couldn't help himself and burst into tears. His wife, who was taking notes, was stunned. She'd never seen him cry like that . . . ever.

Master Zhang explained, "We've got to do a ceremony" and told Sam what she would need for a fire ceremony later that evening on the beach in order to release his mother's spirit. Then, she left, and Master Bruce Sun started working on Sam.

Highly skilled in martial arts, tai chi, and qigong, Master Bruce had also learned his own unique way of working with people's energy through hands-on healing. His method is complicated, but he starts by scanning a person's body with his hands to pick up on their energy and to basically *read* the person's body. His hands will often get very hot when he does this. So, Master Bruce asked Sam to lie down on a bed and Master Bruce started out the session reading Sam's energy with his hands. When his hands got to Sam's liver area, he began pushing deep into the tissues of the liver and massaging Sam's stomach toward his liver.

Master Bruce identified where the angry little boy was and told Sam, "He's in your liver . . . he won't let go . . . and he doesn't want to come out." The deep massaging was extremely painful for Sam but also seemed to release emotional pain, and Sam began to cry again. He felt that Master Bruce Sun was digging into and releasing very old energy of some type. In fact, it felt like it was all the emotional pain and anger that Sam had suppressed over his entire life. Master Bruce also felt this energy in Sam's liver was from when he was a young boy, and Sam intuitively knew it was his own pent-up anger and frustration from childhood. Remarkably, he also felt this energy move and even push back against Bruce's hands. Master Bruce kept pressing deeper and deeper into Sam's abdomen to try to get the tenacious angry energy to release, but to no avail. At one point, Master Bruce leapt back and exclaimed, "Oh, my God—it's a *beast!*"

Sam was crying the whole time and really wanted this energy *out* of him, so he was also telling it, "Get out! Get out!" After more body work, Master Bruce finally felt all the energy was gone and he stopped digging into Sam. But Sam said he could feel the energy was still there. So Bruce worked on him some more until Sam sensed the energy—which felt like a ball of fire at times—was completely gone. Remarkably, at this point, Sam could not get in touch with any of his old anger even when he *tried* to remember it!

Later that afternoon, Sam and his wife went to the local market to collect what would be needed for the fire ceremony. They bought all the items his mother had demanded—a new dress, cake, vodka, cigarettes, garden seeds, and $150,000 in play money. They also moved a big tub onto the beach to build a fire in. Master Zhang put the money in the fire along with all the other items and poured the alcohol in as well. She burned everything in a fire ceremony right there on the beach and, once again, Master Bruce interpreted everything she said. Master Zhang informed them all, "She wants more alcohol and money, and she doesn't know if she wants to do this." She then said forcefully to the spirit of the mother, "You agreed to this . . . and we can help you."

Finally, after working hard to convince the mother's spirit to leave, Sam pulled the shirt off his back and threw it, along with his shoes, into the fire to get rid of every possible connection to her. At long last, the ceremony was successful and Sam actually felt his mother's spirit leave him and move on. Master Zhang's impression was that, given his mother's determination to kill him, if they were *not* able to release her spirit, Sam probably would not live more than seven more years.

Sam would never have guessed this day would be so intense or such a pivotal point in his life. All he knew was that he was grateful he had made the trip and been able to work with Master Zhang and Master Bruce! And after leaving Mexico and returning home, he easily lost thirty pounds with little effort and felt that stressful things did not bother him as much as before. He felt all his past anger, frustration, and hate had been truly cleared from him!

Snakes Seek Revenge

But Sam's session with Master Zhang had been even more epic than so far described because, not only did she deal with his mother's vindictive spirit, but she also found the spirits of some very determined snakes around Sam—and they were out for revenge.

According to Master Zhang, there were two poisonous snake spirits around Sam and another big, non-poisonous snake. These were snakes Sam had killed on his ranch and they were very, very angry at him. Sam recalled the events. Years before, he had noticed two poisonous water snakes in his pond that he killed to protect his children and others on the property. And, at a different time, he had tried to remove a non-poisonous four- to five-foot snake from inside his ranch house. He had initially tried to simply move the large snake with a mop to the outside, but it was very aggressive and kept trying to get back into the house. It also kept striking at him. So, finally, Sam killed it. Now, in this session with Master Zhang, Sam was discovering that killing snakes was *never* a good idea, no matter what the circumstance.

Master Zhang says that snakes are one of the animals most likely to try to take revenge from the spirit world and, as she had seen in other cases she'd treated in China, the type of revenge they often inflict is blindness. Master Zhang said that Sam, himself, was too strong a target for them to impact, so the snakes had gone after some of his children.

Well, this hit home with Sam because Tim, one of his adult sons, was going blind due to diabetes. In fact, Tim had already had twelve surgeries on one of his eyes and some surgery on the other eye as well. And one of Sam's other adult sons, Jared, had less than a year earlier been drinking and socializing with a friend at Sam's ranch and decided to dive head first into the very pond that the two poisonous snakes had lived in before Sam killed them. The unfortunate result was that Jared broke his neck. Strangely, diving into this pond was a very unusual thing for Jared to do, because he'd always told his friends that no one swims in that pond because there are poisonous snakes in it. Yet, he dove in without a care and even pinned his arms back at his sides—which was why his head hit the bottom of the pond and he broke his neck. Later, Jared would tell his family that he didn't know why he did it except that he had felt inexplicably drawn to dive into that pond.

Master Zhang revealed in Sam's session that it was one of the snake spirits that had caused Jared to dive into the pond. But, when it saw that the damage to Jared's spine would kill him, the snake spirit apparently felt that amount of damage was too much. So it healed some of Jared's bones immediately to reduce the injury. Doctors commented later that Jared's neck was so badly broken, he should have died or at least been completely paralyzed. In fact, they were totally amazed at the swift and full recovery Jared made.

As for the large snake that had been inside the ranch house, Master Zhang said it had been there to bring good luck and fortune to the family and that it had a long, five-hundred-year lineage and was well on its way to evolving into a dragon. So, for those reasons, the big snake was extremely angry that its life had been cut short. Master Zhang had to do some very involved ceremonies to appease and release all three snake spirits and make them move on so they would not bother Sam or his family anymore.

Tumor Jumps Into Hand

Helen came to see Master Zhang as her last hope for a miracle. She had been feeling ill for many years, but none of the numerous doctors or nutritionists she'd consulted were able to help her. None of them could even tell her what was wrong with her. Finally, she saw a brilliant female internist who was able to diagnose her quickly and accurately. Helen had a type of neuroendocrine cancer that had metastasized and spread to multiple organs.

After blood tests and scans were done, Helen was told she had a tumor at the head of her pancreas, a tumor in her liver, and masses in her ilium (pelvic bone) and colon as well. The official medical conclusion was that not all of these tumors were malignant, but some definitely were. Helen's doctors told her chemotherapy would not work for this type of cancer but that her condition was probably curable through surgery. So, a date for surgery was set and the plan was that they would remove as much of the cancer as they could from all areas, with the tumor in the liver being the one the doctors were most worried about. Helen was relieved to finally know what was wrong with her, but she was also very worried that she would die on the operating table because it would be such an extensive surgery.

Before the scheduled surgery date, an acquaintance of Helen's suggested she see Master Zhang. Helen was skeptical and cautious but, at the same time, a little hopeful. She was committed to going through with the surgery but decided to see if Master Zhang could help her in some way first. Luckily, Helen was able to get some session appointments. In the first session, Master Zhang accurately saw all the cancer that had been diagnosed, and while she scanned Helen's body, Helen noticed a subtle sensation as if she could feel Master Zhang somehow inside her. During the remainder of the session and a second follow-up session, Master Zhang did a lot of energy work on Helen.

Helen admits that she didn't notice any significant difference after these first two treatments. It was during the third session, however, that something quite amazing happened. Master Zhang was focusing on sending energy to Helen's liver, where the most worrisome tumor was, and as she held her hand over that area, she said in her mind, *Release it, release it.* Suddenly, the tumor jumped out of Helen's body and into Master Zhang's hand! There was no opening in the skin . . . just a few drops of blood on her right side.

This was *not* something Master Zhang had expected, and she was quite unnerved by it and not sure what to do with the tumor in her hand. So someone went into the kitchen and got a container to put it in. Helen's eyes had been closed the whole time, and she kept them closed even though she could tell what had happened by what she was hearing people say in the room.

According to Helen,

> I had my eyes closed while Master Zhang was doing the energy work on me. I noticed a sensation of what you might call 'pressure' in my liver area. Suddenly, people in the room were screaming and exclaiming about what had happened. It was crazy and I could tell what had happened by what everyone was saying. But I didn't want to look at the thing. I didn't want to give it any power, and something in my mind kept saying, *Don't look. Don't look.* So I kept my eyes closed until they put the mass in a container. Finally, I opened my eyes and looked down at my abdomen. I was surprised that I could hardly see any difference between my right side and left side, other than what looked like a little bit of redness on the right.

That was the last session Helen had with Master Zhang and, approximately a month later, she underwent surgery as scheduled. Fortunately, the surgery went well. Although it was a very difficult and lengthy procedure, Helen's surgeon was able to remove the tumors in her pancreas, illium, and intestine. He was quite surprised, however, when he could not find any cancer in her liver!

Helen is extremely grateful for her healing and looks at the entire experience as a threefold miracle. The first miracle was that her internist was able to accurately diagnose her when other doctors couldn't; the second miracle was Master Zhang's energy work on her and the liver tumor jumping out of her body; and the third miracle was the outstanding job her surgeon and his medical team did in removing the rest of the cancer. Helen credits these three people with saving her life and likes to think of them as her "three heroes"!

Jade Turtles Everywhere

One of the ways people can have amazing experiences with Master Zhang is through attending one of her private training workshops. She has done only a small number of these in the United States, but they have all proved to be extremely interesting. For instance, in one workshop that was specifically offered to members of a shamanic group in America, a woman asked Master Zhang if she could feel what it was like to have an herbal pill delivered into her own hand instead of Master Zhang's. Master Zhang cannot do this in every case but, in this case, she was able to have the woman put her hand on top of her own. A pill then materialized into the palm of the woman's hand. The woman jumped when it happened because she felt a strange suction type of sensation that she was not prepared for.

And another attendee claimed that when Master Zhang manifested liquid medicine from the air, which poured from her hands, she could actually hear the sound of the liquid being poured—as if someone in another dimension were pouring it from a vessel into Master Zhang's hands!

But Celeste from the "Headless Demon and Spider Spirit" case may have seen one of the *most* incredible events of all at a private workshop. She described it this way:

> I went to a workshop that Master Zhang was giving. There were about twenty participants and it was her first class in

America teaching the *mudras* (hand signals) and to open everyone's third eye. Master Zhang manifested medicine all around the room for everyone and blessed all the participants. Absorbing everything Master Zhang was teaching was very difficult, but no one seemed to mind since we were all so fascinated by what was happening.

Then, at one point, Master Zhang started to laugh for no apparent reason. She opened her hand, and there was a green jade turtle in her palm! It was about one to two inches across and had a Chinese character inscribed on it. It was incredible. Master Zhang said that this turtle in jade had appeared because there was a powerful 'river spirit' in the room that had come to join them. Everyone was exclaiming in amazement. Then, another jade turtle appeared in Master Zhang's hand! A woman said she wanted to have a turtle, too, and Master Zhang answered, 'Look in your pocket.' There, in her pocket was a third green jade turtle. Next, a man said he wanted a turtle as well. So, Master Zhang tapped on the necklace he was wearing, and a fourth turtle appeared! It just popped into existence, and he had to sort of jump to catch it in his hand before it fell. The green jade turtles kept appearing until there were a total of seven or eight!

According to Celeste, everyone at the workshop was completely overcome with awe and it was a life-changing experience!

— IN MASTER ZHANG'S OWN WORDS —

CHAPTER 17

Interview with Master Zhang

So much of what Master Zhang does is completely foreign to people in the western world and difficult for anyone, anywhere to understand. In this section, Master Zhang explains many of her views on reality, life, and healing. With someone like Master Zhang, it is a rare opportunity and an honor to be able to ask her personal questions, as the author was able to do in this interview. Sometimes, even the most minor aspects of her perspective can be very interesting.

Master Zhang, sometimes people of great talent in China are given the special title "National Treasure of China." Many people think of you as a National Treasure, but you were never officially given that title

by the Chinese government. Do you think if you were a man, you would have been given that title?

No, I don't think it had anything to do with me being a woman. Descriptions like "First Strange Mysterious Woman of the East" and other similar things have been written about me in China by high-level officials, and these have already elevated me as a healer to the national level. Of course, titles are really not important. Usually, whenever anyone asks me if I am a National Treasure of China, I just joke and tell them, "Yes—I'm a Panda!"

Why did you first come to the United States?

A Chinese newspaper group in California invited me to come and lecture. So, I applied for the correct visa and made a visit.

What made you decide to spend more time in the United States after that?

I felt I could have more freedom here. Communism in China restricted me from talking about spirits and Buddhism and doing my work fully. It seemed it would be easier for me to achieve my mission here because of the freedom of speech and because things are more democratic here. Also, I felt I might be more accepted by the general public in the United States.

Interview with Master Zhang

When you changed your first name from "Shuxia" to "Ying," was there any particular reason you chose that first name?

It wasn't actually my idea to change my name or even to choose "Ying." I had a dream one night in which my spirit Master with the white beard and mustache appeared, and he said to me, "You know, I think you should change your name!" I asked him what I should change my name to, and he suggested "Ying." He said it was because the Chinese written character for the name "Ying" is made up of parts with special meanings. He explained that on the left side of the character is the symbol for a dagger, which he said would protect me. Underneath the dagger, he said, is the symbol that stands for "Heaven, Earth, and People Unified." This signified my work. Then, he said that on the right side of the Chinese character for "Ying" is a symbol that stands for "all the time." So, he told me the name "Ying" would be good to have because it represented my mission of unifying people, Heaven, and earth, and because it would protect me always. After changing from "Shuxia" to "Ying," a lot of things in my life started going much better!

You are so connected to the spirit world. Do you see spirits pretty much all the time?

Ever since I can remember, I have always seen spirits. As a child, I noticed that I saw them more often in some situations than in others, such as at funerals. But it wasn't until after I was twenty years old that I began to communicate with them. I still see them a lot and often see them walking among people looking like solid, normal humans. Others think they are just regular people, but I can tell they are spirits in human form.

Do you mean that they are like angels walking among us?

Not exactly. Normally, angels look different to me. When I see angels, they always look like they are between sixteen and eighteen years old, and I see them with wings on them. Both male and female angels have wings when I see them in the United States. But when I see angels in China, only the female angels have wings and the male angels don't. In China, the male angels carry a fan instead of having wings.

Can you say anything about your own spirit guides? For instance, how many do you have?

About 300.

Interview with Master Zhang

That's a lot of spirit guides! What are they like?

Some are very high-level spirit beings, like the Medicine Buddha, Kuan Yin, and my white-mustached spirit Master. But there are all kinds, and they help me in different ways. For instance, the night before I see a person who comes to me for healing, my white-bearded spirit Master often appears to me in a dream and tells me all about the person's problems. So I already know in advance much of what the person's issues are before I see them. This elderly spirit Master is also the one who usually delivers the really big or unusual pills to me, like the gold ones, from the Medicine Buddha. But if even *more* powerful medicine is needed, such as liquid medicine that drips from my hands, then it is usually Kuan Yin who gives this to me. If it is simply "normal" pills or powdered medicine that I grab from the air, then it is usually a small boy who delivers those to me. The medicine always originates from the Medicine Buddha, and there are many guardians involved in delivering it. Some of my spirit guides are animals, too.

Some are animals?

Yes. For instance, there is a snake, a turtle, a fox, a deer, a coyote, and a golden dragon. They all give me information and help me in various ways.

THE DIVINE AND MASTER ZHANG

You mentioned a dragon, and everyone knows dragons are very common in Chinese culture. But, in the western world, we think of dragons as mythical creatures. Are they more than myth?

I can tell you that dragons are real. Once when I was a teenager, I was walking along a path with my mother near some water. I saw a very large animal and realized it was a dragon. My mother did not see it, though, and no one else could see it, either. Only I could see it. As I got close, it spit water all over me and got me all wet! My mother turned around and asked, "Why are you so wet?" I was embarrassed to tell her that a dragon had just spit on me, so I told her I fell in the water. But that dragon spoke to me. It said, "My name is Golden Armor Dragon." I knew this experience was a great honor and a blessing and that it is always good to encounter a dragon. I saw that same Golden Armor Dragon two more times and noticed that my special abilities increased after that.

Are all dragons good? Or are there good and bad dragons?

All dragons are good. There are no bad dragons.

Master Zhang, are you a vegetarian?

No. But I was a vegetarian before I met my teacher and master, the Buddhist nun who rescued me at the train station and taught me to be a healer. At one point, she patted me on my head and told me I should start eating a little meat and seafood at times, and I have done that ever since. But she also told me there are some animals that should *never* be killed for food or for any other reason. Four of these are because they are "highly" spiritual animals, and they are: snakes, turtles, deer, and dogs. The fifth is the ox, because it works so hard to serve man. Dragons are actually snakes that have evolved enough to become a dragon. In China, a person killed a snake once, cooked it, and told me it was fish. As soon as I put it in my mouth, I passed out.

Many people in the United States and other countries often kill deer to eat. Since you say that snakes, turtles, deer, and dogs should never be killed for food, what happens to a person who does this?

A big catastrophe can happen in their business or something like that. If you never harm these very spiritual animals, there will be no problem. And if you protect or help them, they will appreciate that and can do good for you. However, with snakes in particular, if you hurt or kill a snake, they will seek revenge. Sometimes, as is shown in the story of the government official and his wife, they can cause blindness. So it is very dangerous to kill a snake and better to safely relocate it somewhere else if it is poisonous and some action must be taken.

Do you ever see what some people might call "Nature Spirits," such as the spirits of trees, rocks, rivers, flowers, or mountains?

Yes, sometimes. The spirit of the rivers is a turtle, for instance. But nature spirits can take different forms, so they don't always look the same. There are also tree spirits. I see a lot more tree spirits in the United States than in China because there are more trees here since they are protected so strongly by conservation laws.

Can you say more about tree spirits?

Yes, tree spirits can be very helpful to have around. They can protect us against bad spirits, and they can grab good *feng shui* energy from deep underground and bring it up to the surface. So it is best to not cut down trees, if at all possible.

Do your spirit guides help you only with important things like manifesting medicine for healing people? Or do they sometimes help you with little things as well . . . like where you put your car keys?

Oh, yes—they *do* help me with little things all the time. For instance, as soon as I complain, "Where did I put that thing?" it often appears quite quickly somewhere that I can see it easily. Or, if I realize on a particular day that I'm really low on money or that I need something in particular, it will generally show up the next day in some way or other.

Since you see spirits so often and know so many things through your own psychic ability, it sounds like you are always living with one foot in one world and the other foot in another world. I can't imagine how difficult or strange that must be. What does it feel like to be Master Zhang?

I've been asked this question many times. It is not difficult for me. But there are times when my mind just goes somewhere else and people sometimes notice this. It's like they can tell my body is here but my mind is elsewhere. I can usually control this, but not always. Overall, I am just a human being . . . a person in this world. But I am definitely different from most people.

Can you communicate easily with living animals, such as dogs, cats, and horses?

I can easily communicate with any animal that is in spirit after death if it wishes to communicate with me. In general, though, I can't really understand living animals because they don't know the spirit language. Only once in a while can a living animal get a message to me. Pets that have developed a very close bond with their master, such as dogs, sometimes do this. Pets can also become good spirits that protect their owners from the other side. This especially happens in America, where people become very close to their animals.

How do you understand or explain karma?

Karma is a very important law of cause and effect. For instance, if you do good deeds, you will be blessed with good things that will happen.

Is karma usually a result of things done in a past life or in the current life we live?

It is both. A person may experience immediate karmic effects in their current life, or they may experience them in their next life.

You have spoken about "karmic creditors." Can you explain what you mean?

Karmic creditors are basically spirits that collect on karmic debts, and this may be the cause of some illnesses. In my healing work, I can often send these karmic creditors, or collector spirits, away to restore a person's health.

You have generously offered your spiritual healing for most of your life to just about anyone who has sought your help. How much have you done for no charge?

In China, I worked with many people who were poor and could not afford to pay. Also, there were certain categories of patients I would *never* accept money from. They were:

1) The elderly
2) Veterans who've been injured in war
3) People with disabilities

Are there circumstances where you should not help a person to heal?

Yes, I should not use my special abilities to cure small conditions like a cold in family members or friends. When I was young, my siblings used to ask me to do these things and I had to say "No." Also, I should not heal myself. But on the whole, I can and should provide medication treatments to people to help cure their illnesses. The only exceptions are these three categories:

1) Dying of old age
2) Offending Heaven and reason
3) Getting retribution

When you say "offending Heaven and reason," what do you mean? And what does "getting retribution" mean?

"Offending Heaven and reason" is when someone is arguing with me about the existence of spirits or about what I do. It's okay if they are not spiritual people or don't even believe in God. I don't mind that. But if they want to argue with me, then I see that as offending Heaven and reason. "Getting retribution" is when a person has done bad things and karma has made that person sick as a result. However, if the person really wants to change and become a good person, then I will treat him or her.

One of the photographs shows you working with archaeologists who are studying mummies. In what ways were you able to help them?

I was able to tell them some things about how the mummified person lived or what they died from.

I think there might be some archaeologists in the western world who would like to hire you to help them in their work, especially since you can walk around an area and know where ancient artifacts are buried underground. Would you be interested in helping archaeologists in those ways if they were open-minded to your talents?

Yes, possibly, if I have time. I am also open to working with scientists to further the understanding of psychic abilities—but only if their interest is sincere and they are not just trying to prove or disprove psychic phenomena. It would depend on how much of my time it would take, though.

What kinds of lectures, workshops, or other presentations do you want to do in the United States or other countries in the western world?

I want to teach whatever can help people's health. Meditation techniques, for instance. Americans have too much stress. I would also like to be able to help people open up their own abilities. I believe everyone possesses an undeveloped ability to be a healer. I would like to help those people who are interested in developing their own abilities as well as those who are already healers but wish to broaden their skills.

How do you personally explain or think of God?

I see God as the "Commander-in-Chief." He sends all kinds of representatives down. The purpose or message is always only one: We are to be good people, not bad people, and to do good deeds!

Overall, can you sum up what you would like to accomplish or how you want to contribute to humanity in general?

My overall goal is to love all life, to protect all life, including animals, and to give health and happiness as much as I can to those who need it. And I especially want to be able to help or influence those who are in a position to be able to contribute to the world in big ways. This could include healers, scientists, famous people, business leaders, and politicians. This is because, if I can positively influence one person in a position of power to want to do more good, it can help many, many people.

Chapter 18
Mysteries of the Universe

Wave of Life

I HAVE LEARNED MANY THINGS throughout my life as a psychic. For instance, in the universe, all things put out information that reflects their nature. Some of this information can be seen, such as when one sees a tree. Some of it may *not* be seen but can be smelled, such as with the scent of a flower. Many things can be seen, smelled, touched, and heard, yet other things may only be detected through one form of reflection. An example of this might be a blind person who knows someone is coming only by the sound of their footsteps. Everyone is familiar with this and understands there are multiple ways we receive information each and every day.

However, some information cannot be seen, smelled, or touched by ordinary people. This would include information through electromagnetic waves, including certain light waves and acoustic waves. But these forms of information *do* exist and can be detected by the appropriate instruments and apparatuses. For example, the waves transmitted by a television station can be received and interpreted by the electronics within a television set. Once the information is presented on the television screen, then people can see and hear it.

But there is something else. Among the various types of information that all human beings put out, there is something that could be called the "wave of life." It cannot be sensed through normal means, yet it nevertheless transmits information constantly to reveal aspects of a person's health and life. If you have the ability to perceive this wave of life, then you can use it to have an accurate understanding of health.

This wave of life may be strong or not strong and reflects the state of the human being's organs, blood, veins, and nervous system according to that person's condition. Actually, it is really all the information coming from the seven *chakras*. These seven "wheels" can also emit different colors of light. For instance, they may appear as gray, purple, red, yellow, or another color. Each color reveals something about the person. So the life wave provides a lot of information about each of us. It is not the same as "chi," but the chi in the body does support each of the wheels.

Time and Information From the Universe

I think that, to the universe, there is no concept of time. In other words, the present, past, and future are artificial concepts and are merely hypothesized by human beings from the rotation of the earth, sun, and moon. There is only one space, and it is the universe.

Mysteries of the Universe

All things possess two categories of information:

1) Information that transcends time and space as humans experience and understand time and space.

2) Information that does *not* transcend the human understanding of time and space.

The latter can be sensed by everyone, and the former can be perceived only by the psychic with extrasensory perception. Human beings, though the most clever of all creatures on earth, usually cannot understand themselves and cannot utilize all of their own abilities to the fullest. Therefore, most people can only perceive the non-transcending time and space phenomena and information.

But information in the universe is linked together, whether it is in what we perceive as the present, the past, or the future. For many people, this is understandably difficult to conceive of, but for the psychic, it is different. The psychic can perceive the information from the universe in ways that are totally different from the sensory perception people ordinarily use to see, smell, hear, taste, and touch.

The reason I knew the ancient knife-shaped coins were buried underground in Chaoyang City, and how I can know things about a person's past is because the information in the universe is linked together and I can sort through the combination and mixture of this information. With the information provided by the object, one can make an analysis or diagnosis. The more information, the greater the accuracy will be. It is just like when you go to the library to look something up. If you possess more information on the material you are interested in, you may spend less time and have more accurate results.

In other words, when the psychic makes a diagnosis of a person, the more comprehensive the information, the more accurate the diagnosis. That is the *xiang* (the information's comprehensiveness) that can be caught from space by remoteness, from ideology by transmittance, from all the intuitions, and sometimes from obscure pictures. In short, the perception of the psychic is comprehensive.

Psychic powers cannot be taught verbally. They are experiential and all the experiences are in an instant. The real manifestation of psychic powers cannot be easily cultivated except with an insistent, hardworking attitude and a high morality.

Pre-Prediction and Post-Prediction

In the Tang Dynasty, poet Xu Hun wrote a poem, and one of the verses went like this:

> *The wind sweeping through the tower*
> *heralds a rising storm in the mountains.*
> *The rising wind forebodes the coming storm.*

The wind is the omen of the storm. Before the arrival of an earthquake, there are always some omens, too, such as the mice running out from underground cavities or boiling water spraying out. And modern weather forecasting is an example of prediction based on analyzing information in advance of the weather occurrence itself. In a similar way, psychic prognostication depends on the information reflected from the objects predicted, and through mental perception the psychic makes the prediction. Before anything happens, there are always some phenomena appearing or some information disseminated beforehand.

Prognostication through extrasensory perception can be divided into two types:

1) The prediction *before* the occurrence has occurred, which is then proven later by facts. We may call this "pre-prediction."

2) The prediction *after* the occurrence has occurred (such as knowing details about how a person received an earlier injury). We may call this "post-prediction."

People often doubt the pre-prediction, though they may believe the post-prediction, especially those things that happened which no one knows about except the person concerned. So, after the acceptance of post-prediction, people should also welcome the pre-prediction and naturally change their doubtful attitude toward psychic powers. Some people are afraid of the psychic's straightforward predictions because they will lose all their secrecy. This is especially true of greedy people.

As for the information, sound, pictures, or implications I receive when I start using my psychic abilities, I cannot give any explanation of them. I think maybe this is an important problem to be explored because, even though I have psychic powers, I myself cannot understand, scientifically, how they are done. However, I think it is a process of transmitting and accepting information. I can perceive information from the universe that most people cannot sense, or they may have only the slightest sense of but cannot accept.

Three factors have contributed to my psychic powers:

1) My congenital inheritance—including my grandfather, father, and mother with her experience of delivering me at birth.

2) My diseases and disasters—including the tornado with the nail and three suicide attempts.

3) The natural environment I grew up in—including geological features. (In my hometown, there are four more female psychics like me.)

Besides the above, my consistent practice of the powers taught to me by my Master is also important.

I do perceive information from the universe very well, and take the information that is transmitted according to what I need. As for the information source, I think omnipotent elements of information do exist and keep up the everlasting transmission while transcending time and space as we know it and penetrating through all obstacles.

The modern sciences are basically the "macro-sciences," and they have difficulty interpreting the "micro-phenomena" that are much more wonderful than the macro-phenomena. In the near future, the truth of so-called mysterious phenomena, or currently unexplained psychic powers, will be discovered and understood.

Bioelectric Current (Chi)

Life exists in balance. If the natural environment, social circumstances and/or living conditions heavily impact this balance, then diseases inevitably occur. This impact mainly comes from human beings themselves. I use my psychic powers to change the imbalance of the human body back into harmonious balance.

The source of every human body's energy is bioelectric current, which many know as chi. It is a unique, pulsating current that travels through the *jing luo*, or invisible channels of the body for nerve and energy communication (acupuncture meridians). This bioelectric current performs the functions of transmittance and acceptance for maintaining the balance of the body. It is the system of biological activities we are born with and, in order to sustain life, the human being must first guarantee the current of this congenital system. If the postnatal current is overly consumed in the nerve system, the supply of current from the congenital system will be greatly injured and result in biological imbalance. That is why the human body gets diseases. However, each person does not like to give up the lifestyle he or she is accustomed to and most people cannot help but to live and work somewhat involuntarily. Thus, here come the various diseases.

The bioelectric current may also be used insufficiently because of the non-starting condition of the brain cells. It is a type of self-protection for the human body. But the bioelectric current of the psychic is different from that of ordinary people. At present, most human beings cannot increase this bioelectric current through their own efforts, whether voluntarily or involuntarily. However, it can be done through special means, such as strong stimulation or special cultivation. That is why I meditate before performing psychic powers. I cannot explain why meditation is necessary, but only by entering into meditation can my psychic powers be started.

The Holographic Cell

The human being's cell is a miniature for the whole body, and the whole human body is holographically linked to the whole universe. The human body and the universe can communicate. The holographic law of the universe can combine with the holographic law of the human body, and they can also be separated from one into two. There is a type of force in the universe that can influence every human being, especially the ideology of human beings. It is a regular motion with law, a substantial movement influencing society, family, and individuals. Through this law, one's balance will be reached.

The universe needs balance, and the human body needs balance, too. If the *yin* and *yang* in the body become disordered and the law of balance is sabotaged, the human being shall get disease. The holographic law proves that the universe is full of informative feelings, and everyone is continuously transmitting informative feelings to the universe and receiving informative feelings from the universe, not only at the time of living, but also at the time after death.

Idea Moving (Teleportation)

Moving things by psychic powers is to move things from a distance without physical contact with those things. In English, this may be referred to as psychokinesis or teleportation. Only by psychic powers can something be moved to another place according to the psychic's need. This kind of moving can be called *idea moving*.

The idea information transmitted by the psychic has a certain direction pointing to the object region. Moving things by idea force can be realized even over distances of more than ten thousand li (about 3,500 miles). When a psychic with the power of idea moves things, the process will not be sensed by people. The velocity of motion is extremely fast and can pass through any obstacle, whether it is time or space. The average person usually does not admit the existence of this type of motion because it is an extrasensory form of moving.

Someone may make a joke and say: "Zhang Ying, if you can move things by psychic powers, then why not move all the money from the bank into your home? You could be a billionaire!"

Of course I *have* moved money and made it appear unexpectedly at demonstrations. But to keep it would be wrong. I can say that, according to normal logic, it seems like this would be possible. But, to a psychic, it is not the proper way of acting and would be a *big* mistake if he or she were to try to do something like that. Why? Because psychic powers should not be misused. It is just like with a high official. They have political power that should not be misused. If it is misused, their selfishness will result in corruption and they shall be punished. The psychic cannot perform extrasensory perception in a way that opposes the law of nature, virtue of the universe, and social morality. If the psychic has committed that mistake, or even thought about it, then their psychic powers will be completely eliminated. It is a serious wrong, and the heavens shall bring severe punishment on the psychic.

It is also important to understand there is more than just my own mind involved in idea moving. My guardian spirits also play a role. In other words, it is my own mind that decides what I want moved and where I want something moved to, but it is the guardian spirits who move it.

More About "Strange Things"

As for the *strange things* and getting rid of ominous information or the residual informative feelings, I have given my description and comments in previous pages. (An example is the hammer covered in mud left in a home by a workman who had been injured or killed.) The so-called "strange things" are things that damage the energy flow *(qi chang)* of an area. They transmit ominous informative feelings and cause residents of these areas to suffer an imbalance of *yin* and *yang*. This imbalance is also related to the art of *Feng Shui* (pronounced "Fung Shway"). If the residents are weak in their immune protection and living in a place with damaged energy flow, then they will fall ill.

Strange things were actually talked about centuries ago. Ji Xiaolan was a well-known scholar and high imperial official of the Qing Dynasty. In *Anecdotes of Yuewei Hermitage*, he recorded a story about how strange things in one home caused the heads of three generations of families to die of heart disease due to insomnia. Finally, the head of the fourth generation asked advice from a Feng Shui Master. This Master discovered there was a niche with old lamp stands causing an imbalance of the energy in the house. After getting rid of the strange things that were blocking the energy flow, the recurring illness was naturally eliminated. Ji Xiaolan commented that strange things such as this could affect the life and death of human beings, and he saw it as a fact to accept.

The reason I can perceive those strange things, as well as rare prescriptions, is essentially that I have psychic powers endowed by nature, which loves life. *Nature takes advantage of my psychic powers to free people from pain and suffering.*

Chapter 19
Strange Prescriptions

—m—

WHILE IN CHINA, I sometimes received *rare and strange prescriptions* through my psychic powers to help me cure difficult or complicated cases. Some of these unusual medication treatments came to me through dreams, and some appeared on my mental screen in the form of language, pictures, or implications to provide me with the information I needed. I have a notebook written with figures, pictures, lines, and dots. No one can read it except me. If anyone asks me about it, I say, "It's the heaven book with rare and strange prescriptions to cure difficult and complicated diseases." All the prescriptions are sent by my heavenly masters, and all are very effective.

Wild Scorpions to Cure Stomach Cancer

In late November of 1994, a fifteen-year-old boy in the Liaoning Province named Wang Bing had become very thin because he vomited whenever he tried to eat. On December 21, he was taken to a hospital for treatment and was found to have cancer. A tumor was evident in his throat and the diagnosis was "carcinoma of the smooth muscle of the esophagus." The boy was scheduled for surgery. The surgery was exploratory and numerous tumors were also then found in his stomach.

After the initial surgery, Wang Bing was taken to the Beijing Academy of Medical Science for examination. The final diagnosis was that he had a terminal case of stomach cancer and probably had no more than three and a half months to live. The hospital had exhausted all medical options for the teenager, so his parents were told to take him home and begin funeral preparations.

On January 4, 1995, Wang Bing's family heard I was coming to their area to give a public lecture on psychic powers and give healing demonstrations. So, with one final effort of hope, they carried him to the lecture hall to see me.

As usual, Lucky Cards were distributed, but Wang Bing did not get one. However, his father would not be stopped. He carried the boy on his back to the stage. The boy was just skin and bones by then and weighed only thirty kilos. Wang Bing's father got down on his knees and begged me for kindness, pleading, "Please save my son."

Soon, the whole audience was shouting, "Please save him!" They pitied the young boy and had a strong desire that he be helped. I was moved as well, and I determined to help him as an exception, even though he did not have a Lucky Card. After my examination, I said, "I know the boy has been through an operation. But this operation did not cure his cancer. It is still in his esophagus and stomach and is very serious. According to medical terminology, it is terminal cancer and should end his life."

Strange Prescriptions

Both the boy and his father were in tears as they heard my diagnosis. Many in the audience were in tears, too. Someone called out, "Master, please save the boy!"

I was so moved I started my psychic powers to make up medicine for the boy. However, as much as I tried, the medicine would not come. I was perspiring anxiously and thought, *I must save the boy. If I can't, I'll give up my mission of making up medicine from the air.* I made up my mind and started walking around the stage. Finally, the medicine came. It was a black pill. The entire theater was ringing with applause!

But Wang Bing had a concerned look on his face and said to me, "I'm afraid I will vomit. If I vomit, the medicine will be wasted."

I assured him, "Child, you can eat it. You will not vomit this medicine." I took a bowl with water and helped the boy take the black pill. I then told him, "After taking this medicine, you can let your mother boil millet gruel for you and you should be able to eat it easily. You will not vomit that, either."

Later that night, Wang Bing's father brought him back to the theater for the evening gathering and reported to everyone, "After taking the master's medicine, my son did not vomit. He was even hungry and ate a bowl of millet gruel and egg soup. He did not vomit after those, either!"

I said, "Very good. The boy has a chance for recovery now," and I made up some more medicine from the air for him.

The two pills had stopped Wang Bing's vomiting, but to cure the cancer completely, he needed a special prescription. A secret prescription appeared on my mental screen and I explained it to the father. This prescription was rare and required that the parents do the following: "Use scorpions dipped in heavy sauce; bake and grind them into powder, and take the powdered medicine by mouth." The family prepared this prescription precisely as told and gave it to the boy.

After another six months, Wang Bing was taken to the hospital for examination again. The doctors were surprised, because the tumors in his esophagus and stomach were much smaller. In fact, they were nearly gone. Wang Bing's father said, "It was Master Zhang who cured Wang Bing's cancer with a rare prescription."

In November of 1996, the whole family visited me in Shenyang. Wang Bing was tall and healthy looking by then, and you could not tell he'd been dying of cancer two years before. Eight years later, I received an invitation to his wedding, which I attended. He had changed his name to "Wang Wei" after being cured of terminal cancer. He did this because "Bing" means "ice," and he'd had tumors in his stomach, where the stomach *yin* is already designated as cold. *Wei* means "great" or "grand" and has a lot of *yang* energy in it. Also, because he almost died, the name change symbolized that he had become a new person.

Seven-Star Spiders to Cure Cancer

On November 2, 1996, I was invited to give a high official the medication treatment. He sent a car to pick me up, and the driver, who was a young second lieutenant just out of military medical school, was the family doctor. The high official's wife had cancer and the chemotherapy that had been given to her had caused her pain and made her hair fall out. They wanted to know if I could help her. So I started my medication treatment and was able to make up medicine from the air to control the wife's illness. But I said to the family,

Strange Prescriptions

"Her illness is very difficult to cure unless we can find some special medicine for her. That is the information I got with my extrasensory perception."

The family members eagerly asked, "What is the special medicine?"

I replied slowly, one word at a time, as it came to me: "Seven . . . Star . . . Spider!" Then, I explained that, "This spider is very difficult to find, so I will send some people to search for it in the villages. If it is found, then the patient might have a chance to live. If not, then the illness cannot be cured. That is the destiny."

By chance, on the second day, one of the men who went to the village to look for the spider called me, saying he had caught some spiders and would return with them the next day. I asked him, "Are you sure they are Seven-Star spiders?" He said, "No problem!" I replied, "Ah, the patient gets her chance."

On the fourth day, the spiders arrived and were put in a small box. I said to the man, "Be careful. They are very poisonous!"

I looked at the spiders to make sure they were what we needed. I then showed them to the patient's family and said, "You see? It is a tiny spider, and on its back are seven white dots. No more, no less. Each of them has the seven dots."

At that time, the young man who'd caught the spiders said, "It was very difficult to find those spiders. I visited many places, and it wasn't until I asked the old villagers and they guided me to a dilapidated house that I found them."

I asked the second-lieutenant driver to prepare the necessary materials and utensils, including one egg. The process was to make a small hole in an egg, insert a Seven-Star spider into the egg and then seal the hole with mud. Next, I instructed them to bake the egg in the ashes of millet sticks. Then, I suggested they ask the patient to eat the egg without mentioning the contents. Once the egg has been eaten, one should observe the patient carefully.

The official's wife ate the egg at noon, and two hours later, she had a fever and loose bowels. The second-lieutenant driver came to me and told me the situation. I said, "Don't worry! It's good. It means she is dispelling the poison." So I put on my overcoat and went to the woman's house by car. In her house, I re-performed my psychic powers toward helping her use the poisonous spider to get rid of the cancer. At the same time, I made up one more batch of medicine for her.

Afterward, the woman's cancer was completely eliminated.

Later, the second-lieutenant driver asked me how I had learned how to prepare the rare prescription. I told him: "When I finished the medication treatment for the official's wife and got back home, the white-mustached old man who is my spirit Master and teacher came to me in a dream. The old man told me the patient should have the Seven-Star spider as the medical therapy. I asked about the process and he told me to watch the scene. Then a group of children dressed in old-style clothing appeared. They showed me the entire process, including how to make the hole in the egg, how to squeeze the spider into the egg, and how to bake the egg in the hot ashes of millets. I watched them, one scene after another, just like watching a movie."

I also explained, "Whenever I have difficult and complicated illnesses, my mental screen will always show such scenes automatically. It is a way of teaching me the skill and the methods as well. Sometimes, the teaching process shows in writing and sometimes by pictures or implications. All prescriptions are effective."

Strange Prescriptions

I do not know how all the scenes happen, and I cannot interpret them scientifically. If science can provide an explanation and interpretation, then I believe it will greatly benefit the development of society and the progress of science and technology as well.

Bronze Thimble to Cure Epilepsy

When I was thirteen years old and lived in my older brother's house in Lanzhou in the Gansu Province to receive more education through homeschooling, I helped my sister-in-law take care of her six-year-old son, who had epilepsy. When the boy had seizures, he drooled white saliva and his belly became bloated. I felt sorry for him when I saw him going through this and was always thinking about how to cure him. Once while I was thinking about him, a strange method suddenly came to me. It seemed that someone was telling me: *You can put a bronze thimble on your finger and insert it into the child's anus several times, letting the air blow out. In this way, the illness should be cured.*

I told this to my older brother and sister-in-law with confidence and satisfaction, but they did not appreciate my suggestion. On the contrary, my brother stared at me and said, "Don't say such a stupid thing!" And my sister-in-law said, "Girl, what nonsense are you telling us?"

The next day, my sister-in-law went shopping and met an old woman on the street. They chatted. My sister-in-law said something about her son's epilepsy, and the old woman told her, "I have a secret prescription inherited from my ancestors, and it is very effective in curing epilepsy." So, of course, my sister-in-law quickly asked, "Please let me know what it is!" The old woman replied, "Okay. But it is a secret. I pity your sick child, so listen to me, but don't tell anyone else." My sister-in-law promptly promised to tell no one else.

Then, the old woman described the secret prescription. My sister-in-law realized the prescription was basically the same as what I had told her the day before. She was surprised but didn't tell the woman she had already heard of this before. When she returned home, her son was just starting to go into seizures. Without hesitation, my sister-in-law did what the old woman told her. Her boy's illness was cured. It was really a miracle!

At that time, being just thirteen years old, I did not yet understand that I was psychic and that the medication prescription that had come to me was through extrasensory perception. The old woman on the street was there to help me realize what I could do.

Other Prescriptions From Heaven

Some other strange prescriptions that have been sent to me that I have used are: an almond core to cure swollen brain, pig bladder with red-skin garlic to cure diabetes, grape juice and egg to cure pollen allergy, cactus and sour vegetables to cure toothache, and many more. These rare prescriptions are all natural therapies, and their applications are unique, not prepared the same for everyone. As for the source of the information, I do not understand this and have no explanation. If scientists want to research this, I will cooperate with them.

CHAPTER 20

The Work Continues

—m—

Global Connections

MASTER ZHANG CONTINUES to do her healing work in many countries. She has clients in the United States, Japan, Taiwan, Indonesia, and Hong Kong, as well as in other areas of the world. And, of course, she makes numerous trips from California to China every year for healing requests in her home country. Many of her clients in China are government officials, and often the appointments are for follow-up energy work with people she has already helped so they can continue to maintain their health.

Master Zhang has been very involved in philanthropic work as well, particularly in China. For instance, when one of the deadliest earthquakes of all time hit the Sichuan Province of southwestern China on May 12, 2008, she donated forty tons of rice to the victims. Called the Great Wenchuan Earthquake, more than 87,000 people were killed, and many thousands more were missing or injured.

Master Zhang has also donated financial support to certain temples and other good causes in China.

Spiritual Healing in the United States

Different countries have different laws governing healing practices and these must always be taken into account and followed. However, it is also important to understand that what Master Zhang does is completely different from what western countries consider to be medical treatment. A brief look at the bigger picture of spiritual healing reveals that, for thousands of years, societies all over the globe have had healers to help those who were sick. These healers have generally used herbs and other natural substances to help the body heal itself along with prayer and a spiritual belief system upon which the healing approach is based. The spiritual aspect of this type of healing work is often the most important part, and this is certainly true in Master Zhang's case. Without meditation, prayer, the reciting of sutras, and help from the spirit realm, she could not do what she does.

As to the pills, powders, and liquids that she can grab from the air, these are spoken of as "medicine" in Asia because there is a long tradition of referring to herbal or even spiritual treatments as medicine in that part of the world. But in the United States, the word *medicine* has a somewhat different meaning. Medicine and drugs tend to be defined in the western world as substances prescribed to treat specific illnesses or diseases. Master Zhang does not prescribe herbs, drugs, or pharmaceuticals to treat specific conditions. In truth, she does not even know whether a powder or pill, or what type of pill, will materialize out of the air until just before it appears.

That is the decision of the Medicine Buddha, Kuan Yin, or others in the spirit realm. What materializes is herbal in nature for the long-term benefit of helping to balance and support a person's body so the body can heal itself. This is a concept upon which traditional Chinese medicine is based and why practitioners of acupuncture in the United States can legally recommend and provide herbs that complement the acupuncture treatments.

One very interesting question, in fact, is how much of the healing nature of the pills, powders, or liquids manifested by Master Zhang is even due to their herbal content. She has stated that an important aspect of the medicine is actually spiritual, and a person does not even need to ingest it for it to help the body. According to Master Zhang, the herbs she manifests will work just as well if the person *wears them close to their body*, such as in a pouch hanging from their neck, or in a pocket. In the United States, this is what she recommends.

Moreover, Master Zhang keeps no supply of herbs at all. She does not buy herbs, stock herbs, or charge for herbs. She charges only for spiritual healing sessions. If pills, powders, or liquids are indicated to help a person's body recover, they materialize out of the air directly from the spirit realm. Master Zhang is also a high-level energy worker. She often moves and balances energy in people and uses her formidable psychic vision to see details of what needs balancing within the body. And, as has been shown, she often removes spirit attachments to help a person heal. When one takes all of this into account, as well as her ability to psychically receive rare and strange prescriptions from the spirit realm, it is clear that there is almost no end to the variety of things she can do in her healing work.

Master Zhang can help people in another way, too. Just watching her bring about the materialization of herbs or other objects from the air is a life-changing experience. For many, it has the ability to suddenly expand their view of reality and open them up to new possibilities. She can also teach the Chinese Divine Powers, and has an interest in helping other healers broaden their abilities in general.

Over the coming years, Master Zhang hopes to expand her involvement with all aspects of healing and help further the scientific understanding of paranormal phenomena. She explains,

> In the vast universe, phenomena such as psychic powers do exist and should be recognized. Only by understanding, can the wrong path be avoided. One should not deny the existence of something one has not seen or heard, or something one does not yet understand. There is no greater foolishness than when a person does not believe things that do exist and draws a hasty conclusion to resolutely veto them.
>
> People are always trying to understand, develop, and utilize nature as well as themselves. They try to reform nature and consistently disregard psychic powers on earth. The twenty-first century will be the era of *life science and life technology*. It will be the epoch of great breakthroughs in natural science. Through the development of education, the popularization of scientific knowledge, the enhancement of scientific spirit, the reform of scientific methods, and the search for truth, we shall face the challenges of the new century.

Indeed, as Master Zhang predicted, the twenty-first century may turn out to be "The Era of Life Science and Technology." With more understanding of supernormal powers and healing abilities, more understanding about reality in general may be achieved. In allowing her story to be told, Master Zhang is hoping to open the door for sharing what she knows with the world to further this sort of increased understanding. Thus, we could be at the beginning of a truly fascinating time!

APPENDIX

Curious Similarities
A Brief Comparison of Paranormal Abilities

―⚭―

Special Gifts

THE PARANORMAL FEATS Master Zhang performs in her healing work are not always easy to accept and can deeply shake a person's sense of reality. Some may even attempt to deny what she does—claiming, instead, that it must be sleight of hand somehow. Others may claim their religion is against what she does, yet ignore important aspects of their religion in doing so. For instance, some Christians may be leery of Master Zhang's special gifts because they think Christianity does not allow for them. But the Bible clearly speaks of "Gifts of the Holy Spirit" in a way that supports virtually all of what Master Zhang does. Specifically, in 1 Corinthians 12, scripture states:

> There are different kinds of gifts. But they are all given by the same Spirit. There are different ways to serve. But they

all come from the same Lord. There are different ways to work. But the same God makes it possible for all of us to have all those different things. The Holy Spirit is given to each of us in a special way. That is for the good of all. To some people the Spirit gives the message of wisdom. To others the same Spirit gives the message of knowledge. To others the same Spirit gives faith. To others that one Spirit gives gifts of healing. To others he gives the power to do miracles. To others he gives the ability to prophesy. To others he gives the ability to tell the spirits apart. To others he gives the ability to speak in different kinds of languages they had not known before. And to still others he gives the ability to explain what was said in those languages. All of the gifts are produced by one and the same Spirit. He gives them to each person, just as he decides.

But even without the support of religious scripture, there is already a very important body of evidence that supports what Master Zhang does as legitimate, and it has been etched into the records of history. History is replete with examples of special individuals who have displayed amazing healing and paranormal abilities—abilities that obviously have *curious similarities* to those of Master Zhang. Moreover, in taking a closer look, one finds that each of these individuals has used their special gifts for doing good deeds and helping their fellow man.

Spiritual and psychic adepts with unusual abilities have been born all over the world since time immemorial. And they've also lived in modern day as well. In the modern western world, we tend to hear mostly about special individuals in either India or China, because these are two large countries where unusual abilities have long been accepted. For an excellent presentation of the special gifts of many adepts in India, the *Autobiography of a Yogi* is a classic book written by Paramahansa Yogananda. Yogananda was a famous spiritual teacher himself and lived in the United States for many years, where he established a far-reaching meditation movement. For an excellent presentation of people with special paranormal gifts in China, Paul Dong has written several very intriguing books. For example, in his book, *China's Super Psychics*, Dong reports on a wide variety of children who naturally displayed extreme paranormal abilities. Paul Dong refers to what he calls "Exceptional Human Functioning," or EHF, as one of the major mysteries of the world, and his own research is a great contribution to the study of this mystery.

However, Europe and the Americas have also contributed incredible examples of special people with "curious similarities" to Master Zhang, many of whom westerners have never heard of. But before looking at some of these special individual healers, one unusual phenomenon deserves mention. This is the phenomenon of levitation. Levitation is *not* one of Master Zhang's abilities, but this phenomenon bears mentioning because it was displayed by her teacher, the Buddhist nun who levitated above her bed every night as she slept. It is therefore a part of Master Zhang's astonishing story.

Levitation

It might surprise a lot of people that there are countless saints in the Catholic tradition who were known to levitate. The terms "Charisms" and "Charismatic Gifts" refer to a variety of extraordinary spiritual gifts that are officially recognized by the Catholic Church, and levitation is actually one of the *most frequently mentioned* of all the charismatic phenomena in the lives of saints. Reportedly, there are hundreds of accounts of saints and other holy ascetics who levitated, including St. Teresa of Avila, St. Francis of Assisi, St. Maria of the Passion, St. Ignatius of Loyola, St. Gemma of Galgani, Padre Pio of Pietrelcina, and many, many more.

But the saint who may have been *best* known for levitation was St. Joseph of Cupertino, Italy, who lived from 1603 to 1663. St. Joseph of Cupertino was said to not only rise up high into the air but also to "be carried away by God" quite a distance at times. Pope Urban VIII once bore witness to this levitation when St. Joseph of Cupertino visited Rome for the first time and went with the Father General to see the Pope. While bending down to the feet of the Pontiff, the saint became so enraptured, he rose in the air and hovered there until the Father General commanded that he return. On another occasion, St. Joseph went into a church in Assisi to visit a well-known religious statue. As soon as he entered and looked at the statue of the Immaculate Conception high up on the altar, he reportedly flew over the heads of everyone there and hovered in the air in front of the statue for a while, before flying back to where he had first been standing. Yet another time while outdoors, St. Joseph was said to have heard a priest say, "Father Joseph, how beautiful God has made Heaven." The saint was apparently so moved that he flew up to the top of an olive tree and knelt on a thin, uppermost branch for about half an hour. The branch swayed only slightly as if it were supporting no more than a tiny bird. Remarkably, it is said that St. Joseph of Cupertino was observed to levitate on more than one hundred different occasions!

Appendix: Curious Similarities

Strange Prescriptions and Distant Diagnosing

In the history of the United States, there is no American psychic more famous than Edgar Cayce (pronounced "KAY-see"). Cayce grew up in a humble working class home in Kentucky and lived from 1877 to 1945. Though not a priest or monk, Edgar Cayce was a devout Christian and so spiritual by nature that, at the age of six or seven, he became so interested in the Bible that he decided to read it from cover to cover every year of his life. He kept that vow. Then, on one very special day when he was only thirteen years old, a beautiful angel appeared to young Edgar and asked him what he wanted most in life. Edgar told her that, more than anything, he wanted to help others, especially children, who were sick. His life then developed in such a way as to make that wish come true.

Like Master Zhang, Edgar Cayce was naturally very psychic. Even as a child, he spoke to angels and communicated with spirits and the souls of loved ones who had passed on. Then, as a young man, Cayce discovered he had an unusual ability no one around him had ever seen or heard of before. He was able to lie down, usually on a couch, and almost immediately put himself into a deep trance or "sleep." From this state, he was able to diagnose people's ailments with incredible accuracy and then prescribe treatments for those ailments. All of the diagnosing and prescribing he did was in trance, and he never remembered anything he said during the trance state once he woke up. In fact, the things Edgar Cayce said while in trance, that he read from his secretary's transcriptions later, initially shocked him. But his ability to diagnose people in this strange sleep state was absolutely perfect. Edgar Cayce never went past eighth grade in school and certainly had no medical training of any kind, yet doctor after doctor confirmed his diagnoses of physical ailments were accurate in every detail.

At first, Cayce himself did not understand what he did or how he did it, but he later learned the information he accessed came from a universal source of information. Like Master Zhang, many of the treatments Edgar Cayce prescribed were quite unusual or even downright strange. But they worked. For instance, Cayce's own wife, Gertrude, developed a bad case of tuberculosis for which several doctors said there was no hope. In fact, at one point, they felt she might have only a week to live. So, Cayce went into his trance state and prescribed a treatment that no doctor would ever have thought of, nor would he have ever thought of it while awake. The treatment involved making a special mixture of heroin in liquid form to be given in a capsule, then filling a charred barrel with apple brandy and having Gertrude breathe in the fumes. All the doctors that Cayce consulted said the treatment was too dangerous and would not support it. After all the medical experts threw up their hands, Cayce finally found one doctor who would work with him and help him administer the remedy to his wife. Using the unusual treatment Cayce had described in trance, Gertrude's health immediately started to improve, and she soon recovered completely.

Edgar Cayce spent forty-three years of his adult life performing "medical readings" for people who were ill, as well as "life readings." During life readings, Cayce went into the very same trance as during medical readings, however, he gave people information about their purpose in life instead of their health. He also told them about their past lives and karmic issues, and gave them spiritual input. Again, all of these readings were while his conscious mind was asleep. Most

Appendix: Curious Similarities

of the readings were carefully recorded in shorthand and typed up by his secretary, Gladys Davis. They are still preserved by the Association for Research and Enlightenment (A.R.E.) in Virginia and are available for anyone to study. This non-profit organization, which was founded by Edgar Cayce in 1931, has a database of 14,306 of his readings, which is why he is considered the most documented psychic of the twentieth century.

Also like Master Zhang, Cayce astonished people when they realized the person he was diagnosing did not have to be in the same room with him. In fact, he often diagnosed and prescribed treatments for people who were hundreds of miles away. While doing this, Cayce sometimes exhibited evidence that some aspect of his awareness was truly observing the distant location by making amusing remarks such as how beautiful the tree in the person's front yard was, or by commenting on the interior décor of the house.

Fascinating explanations of the nature of reality were also revealed in Cayce's readings from the universal source he connected to. For instance, many people think of the fourth dimension as time. Yet, Edgar Cayce saw the fourth dimension differently, and his understanding may be related to how Master Zhang explains teleportation as "idea moving." According to Herbert B. Puryear, Ph.D., who wrote *The Edgar Cayce Primer*, Cayce once said,

> The fourth dimension has its reality in thoughts and ideas. The third dimension is populated by projections from four-dimensional realities into three-dimensional manifestations.

About a dozen biographies and more than 300 other titles have been written about Edgar Cayce's life and work. The most well-known biography may be the easy-to-read book *The Story of Edgar Cayce: There Is a River* by Thomas Sugrue. Though never rich, Cayce became famous during his lifetime, and many of the people he gave readings to were well-known leaders in their fields, such as Thomas Edison, Woodrow Wilson, Irving Berlin, and George Gershwin.

Miraculous Healings

Some of the healings Master Zhang has facilitated over the years have seemed quite miraculous, such as when she waved her hands in front of the official's wife who'd been blind for twenty years because her husband had killed a snake when he was young. In just moments, her blindness dropped away, and she could see again. Are there other healers who have been able to perform miraculous types of healings? Yes, absolutely. In fact, one healer in modern-day Europe would have to be put at the top of that list because of his extreme miraculous healing abilities.

This very special person was a man named Bruno Groening. Groening displayed such extraordinary healing gifts that it would not be an exaggeration to describe him as a Christ-like healer. He was born in Poland in 1906 and later took refuge in Germany after World War II. He was very active as a healer in the 1940s and 1950s, traveling throughout Germany, Austria, and Switzerland. Groening had such an extraordinary gift of healing that he was called the "Miracle Doctor," and he became a household name in post-war Germany almost overnight.

Bruno Groening's fame caused thousands of people from all parts of the world to flock to him for healing, and he often gave talks in front of very large audiences. One of these talks had to be given outdoors in a vast field to accommodate about 30,000 people. Most of the time, he lectured about how to think, heal, and connect to God. As he did so, miraculous healings in the crowds would occur.

The healings that occurred around Groening were nothing short of Biblical. Since World War II had left behind a sea of people who were hurt, maimed, or disfigured, there were plenty of ordinary individuals desperate for help. As Bruno walked through crowds, people often cried out, asking him to help them with their pain. He would simply turn and look at the person and say, "Where did you say your pain is?" The person would then invariably be dumbfounded because their pain had suddenly disappeared and their condition healed instantly. Even more astonishing, he was known to ask all the blind or deaf people in a crowd to come to the front of the gathering, and he would somehow, in no time at all, take their afflictions away. At one massive gathering, he suddenly turned to a whole row of people in wheelchairs and said something like, "Now, all of you in wheelchairs, please stand up!" At first, no one moved. But he encouraged them and told them they could do it. Soon they were all miraculously walking and pushing their own wheelchairs!

Bruno Groening was always very psychic and even as a child was known to predict things that would happen in the future. And, like Master Zhang and Edgar Cayce, he could diagnose anyone at any distance.

The most common things Bruno lectured about were God, how to receive healing, and the role our thoughts and behaviors play in our health and life. Thus, he was not only a healer, but a great spiritual teacher as well. Luckily, many of his lectures have survived him, and many books have been written about him by people who knew him and/or had interviewed individuals who'd been healed by him. Some of these books and a documentary film are available on Amazon.com, and a search of his name on the Internet will bring up various websites with detailed information.

Rising From the Dead

One of the more unbelievable aspects of Master Zhang's life is the time when she was dead for ten days. Medical science tells us that brain damage due to lack of oxygen may occur in people within a very short time after their heart stops beating. So, coming back to life and being able to function again after being dead for so long is understandably difficult to accept. Indeed, there is no conventional medical explanation for it.

The question is, have there been others besides Master Zhang who were dead for days before being brought back to life? Apparently there have been. For example, one well-documented case was that of the Russian scientist, Dr. George Rodonaia.

Dr. George (Yuri) Rodonaia lived under the heavily suppressive Soviet regime. He was highly educated and held not only an M.D. but two PhDs. Rodonaia worked as a research psychiatrist at the University of Moscow and had a great love for the physical sciences and medicine. He was also an atheist. In the mid-1970s, Dr. Rodonaia was invited to pursue advanced research at Yale University, which put him in a bind. The offer thrilled him, but the KGB would not let him go, fearing he would defect and seek asylum in the United States. Rodonaia had always been outspoken against the communist regime, and he also knew important top-secret scientific information.

Appendix: Curious Similarities

Two years later, however, Rodonaia was married with a baby, and the Soviet government then agreed to let him go as long as his wife and baby stayed home. Unfortunately, the KGB higher-ups had no intention of *really* letting him go, because on the day Rodonaia was scheduled to depart for the United States, he was waiting for a cab to the airport when a speeding car drove up onto the sidewalk straight at him. After swerving to avoid some trees, the car hit Rodonaia head on, causing him to fly about ten meters through the air. Then the car re-maneuvered, headed toward him, and ran over him before driving off.

Dr. Rodonaia was rushed to the hospital where doctors did everything they could to save him. But, unfortunately, they failed, and Rodonaia was pronounced dead. For three days, his body was in a cold-storage drawer in the hospital morgue. Finally, his body was taken out of the cabinet, put on a gurney, and washed so an autopsy could be done. Just as the autopsy doctors started cutting into his abdomen, Rodonaia felt himself being "pushed" back into his body and he opened his eyes. He was quickly transferred to the emergency ward upstairs by the shocked doctors.

Dr. Rodonaia had to stay in the hospital for many months to recover, but he came out of the experience with his full mental faculties. He also remembered in great detail what he'd experienced during the three days he was dead. Like Master Zhang, he was able to watch things happening in the physical world. According to Dr. Rodonaia, in his disembodied state, he visited his family and saw his wife and children grieving his death. He then visited his next-door neighbor, who was also very upset about his death.

But his neighbor had another problem as well. The neighbor's new baby, just a couple days old, would not stop crying, and none of the doctors could figure out why. The baby was hardly able to eat or sleep and was in grave danger of dying. In his spirit form, Dr. Rodonaia found he could telepathically communicate with the baby, and indeed the baby stopped crying momentarily and looked directly at him when he started to "talk" to it. Rodonaia asked the baby what was wrong and psychically got the information that the baby's hip was fractured (possibly caused during its birth). There was nothing Rodonaia could do about it at the time, but after he came back to life a couple days later, he immediately got a message to his neighbor about the fractured hip. Doctors were then able to fix the problem and save the baby's life.

After his three-day death experience, Dr. Rodonaia became a priest in the Russian Orthodox Church and later moved to the United States, where he worked as an associate pastor at a Texas Methodist church until he died in 2004. Interviews of him telling his story in his own words are available via YouTube videos.

Manifesting Objects Out of the Air

Of all the special abilities, or gifts, that Master Zhang has, the one that few have been able to duplicate is her ability to materialize things into three-dimensional reality. One famous spiritual teacher, however, who *was* able to do this was Sai Baba in modern-day India. "Sri Sathya Sai Baba," as he was reverently referred to, was born in 1926 and only recently passed away, in 2011.

Many books have been written about Sai Baba, and they all report countless occurrences of amazing manifestations. Sathya Sai Baba was most well-known for materializations of ash referred to as "Vibhuti." This ash had healing properties and Sai Baba often manifested it and handed it out to the public while walking through the

Appendix: Curious Similarities

huge crowds of people who flocked to him. But he also manifested many other items as well, such as jewelry, sweets to eat, photographs of himself, or other things as needed. Sai Baba's ability to manifest a variety of items *out of the air* was seemingly effortless. The many such gifts he manifested and handed to people were allegedly to strengthen their faith in God and possibly also to help establish a link between himself and his devotees. Sai Baba's life and teachings are quite enlightening and well worth looking into through books and film footage.

What is important to remember is that all of these examples of healers with curious similarities to Master Zhang are merely a *small sampling* of the total number of people with highly paranormal psychic and healing abilities that have been gifts to humanity throughout history. However, by looking at even this small sampling, we see that all these individuals lend credibility to each other. It is easy to discount one example, but how can we discount them all? Especially when so many have been credibly documented and witnessed by thousands of observers.

It is time to accept that these and other special individuals are part of our collective heritage and that they can help us to better understand ourselves and the world we live in.

www.ingramcontent.com/pod-product-compliance
Lightning Source LLC
Chambersburg PA
CBHW020400080526
44584CB00014B/1101